Silent Pilots

Silent Pilots

Figureheads in Mystic Seaport Museum

Georgia W. Hamilton

Mystic Seaport Museum, Mystic, Connecticut 1984

This monograph has been published through a generous grant from the Andrew W. Mellon Foundation.

COVER: *Figureheads on view in the Wendell Building, Mystic Seaport Museum*

Cataloging in Publication Data

Mystic Seaport Museum, Inc., Mystic, Conn.
  Silent Pilots: Figureheads in Mystic Seaport
Museum, by Georgia W. Hamilton.
Mystic, 1984.

  120 p. illus. 26 cm.

1. Figureheads — Mystic Seaport Museum — Catalogs
I. Hamilton, Georgia W., 1943-

VM308.M9

ISBN: 0-913372-30-7
Printed in the United States of America

Contents

Foreword

No other objects evoke such immediate and romantic images of the sea as figureheads. The posture, the often fanciful clothing or lack of it, the eyes searching ahead, stimulate thoughts of far-off lands, exotic ports, and perils at sea. We know that the daily reality of life at sea was seldom as exciting as we sometimes imagine, but we also know that figureheads, survivors from the age of sail, kindle the imaginations of those who see them.

The first Curator of Mystic Seaport Museum, then called The Marine Historical Association, was keenly aware of the impact of these carvings. Carl Cutler worked hard in the 1930s and 40s to develop our figurehead collection and to set a pattern of acquisition that ultimately resulted in the collection here at the Seaport today. Generous donors have contributed either the figures themselves or the resources used in purchasing carvings, and we are indebted to them.

While these bow decorations are of interest by virtue of their form, attire, or artistic merit, they take on far greater significance when they are positively identified with specific vessels. When this information is available there is real substance for interpretation, and the carvings have more meaning for the museum visitor and the scholar. In a number of instances the identity of a figurehead was clearly and accurately established when it was acquired, while in other cases there were vague, unsubstantiated attributions. Over the years, continual research on these figures has resolved a number of questions, confirming some identities, strengthening some attributions, and challenging or dismissing others. The process has been one of constantly building the credibility of our collection.

This book, then, cannot be the ultimate, definitive volume on our figurehead collection but represents the best evidence to date gathered from the most reliable sources. We hope that increased awareness of this internationally important collection will stimulate further interest and research. It was with this intention, to make the collections accessible and to generate scholarship, that the Andrew W. Mellon Foundation made the grant that has supported the publication of this book. We greatly appreciate this contribution.

There are many to thank, donors, curators, photographers, librarians, and editors, but two individuals deserve particular recognition. A talented researcher who has developed a specialization in figureheads, Carol Olsen was employed to carry out the initial work on this project and contributed greatly to its success through her insights and research. The author, Georgia Weyer Hamilton, in her capacity as Head Cataloger in the Museum's Registrar's Office, has been working with this collection for years. She has created a book that will be a reliable source of information for anyone whose imagination has been captured by these sometimes mysterious figures.

J. Revell Carr
Director

Acknowledgments

I WOULD LIKE TO RECORD my appreciation to the institutions and individuals who helped in the preparation of this monograph.

Particular acknowledgment is due Carol Olsen, whose study and examination of the Seaport's figurehead collection formed the basis of this book. I am especially grateful to J. Revell Carr, Director, for his help and encouragement in the early stages of the project, and to Benjamin A. G. Fuller, Curator, for his suggestions, corrections, and comments. I would also like to thank Lloyd McCaffery for reading the manuscript. The design of the book is the work of Paul Gaj.

I am grateful for research assistance and cooperation provided by Kathy Flynn, Peabody Museum, Salem, Massachusetts; Hedy A. Hartman, Museum of History and Industry, Seattle, Washington; Sohei Hohri, New York Yacht Club; Mariners' Museum, Newport News, Virginia; New Bedford Whaling Museum, New Bedford, Massachusetts; Rhode Island Historical Society, Providence, Rhode Island; Sumner Pingree, Jr., Charles Weld Pingree, and John R. Pingree.

At Mystic Seaport I am indebted to William N. Peterson for sharing with me his notes on Mystic shipcarvers Campbell & Colby. In addition, I would also like to give special thanks to Mary Anne Stets and Claire White-Peterson, who photographed the figureheads at the Museum; the Curatorial Restoration staff, David F. Mathieson, Elizabeth L. Parker, Martin F. Hillsgrove, and Elizabeth A. Orzack; the staff of the G. W. Blunt White Library, including the

Manuscripts Division and Archives; Jane Massett, who typed the manuscript; Philip L. Budlong and Richard C. Malley in the Registrar's Office; and in the Publications Department Andrew W. German for bringing to light obscure articles and references. The manuscript could not have been completed without Anne Preuss, project editor. For her constant attention to detail and incredible patience I am very grateful.

Georgia W. Hamilton

Georgia W. Hamilton graduated from Connecticut College in 1966. From 1966 to 1969 she was in the Registrar's Office at the Metropolitan Museum of Art in New York, and from 1970 to 1972 she was Registrar of the Museum of New Mexico. Since 1973 Hamilton has been Head Cataloger at Mystic Seaport Museum.

1. Viking long ship, ca. A.D. 800, discovered at Oseberg, Norway. The reconstructed helical stem with an interlaced dragon design is carved in low relief. Universitets Oldsaksamling, Oslo, Norway, photograph copyright.

Chapter 1

Development of Figureheads from Ancient Times to the Nineteenth Century

THE COLLECTION AT MYSTIC SEAPORT MUSEUM currently comprises nearly seventy figureheads. Most of these carvings came to the Seaport unidentified, with descriptions such as "figurehead of a woman," or "bust figurehead of a man." Some have since been identified through staff research and in at least one instance by an observant visitor to the museum. Many of the carvings came with attributions to vessels that subsequent research has proved spurious or at best inconclusive, and a few have turned out not to be figureheads at all but architectural ornaments or possibly even fakes. This monograph is an effort to impart new knowledge and to correct old misinformation about the collection.

Figureheads were the only major form of shipcarving to last through the nineteenth century. They survived after the decline of lavish ship decoration in the seventeenth and eighteenth centuries, but their design was affected by changes in bow shape as well as by artistic and economic factors. Throughout history hundreds of different kinds of vessels developed, many of which carried some sort of bow decoration, and much has already been written about them and the history of figureheads. But by focusing on the evolution of a few types of sailing vessels in Europe and in the United States it is possible to follow a gradual change in bow configuration and to see how that change affected the shape of figureheads.[1]

Ancient Times

Archaeological remains show that people have decorated their boats for as long as they have been building them. Stone Age rock carvings depict vessels with bows and sterns carved in floral and animal forms. The oldest extant vessel known, an Egyptian funeral boat dating from about 2600 B.C., has a vertical stempost carved in the shape of a papyrus flower. This ship, which was built for the burial of Cheops at Giza, never went to sea, but was intended for the pharaoh in the afterlife (Fig. 2).[2] The Viking long ship discovered at Oseberg, Norway, also a burial vessel, built more than three thousand years later, around A.D. 800, bears reconstructed bow and stern carvings in relief on the upturned ends (Fig. 1). The carvings on these and numerous other early vessels seem to grow from the shapes of the boats themselves, and they undoubtedly held a magical significance beyond the purely decorative.

2. 140-foot burial boat for Cheops, builder of the Great Pyramid at Giza, ca. 2600 B.C. The graceful, upturned bow and stern are integral to the boat's design. Drawn by Kathy Bray.

Europe - Middle Ages to the Nineteenth Century

As Europe entered the Middle Ages trade expanded and seafaring peoples became rivals. Small vessels originally built for peaceful coastal transportation were converted for sea battle. The merchant vessels were equipped with superstructures or "castles" on platforms fore and aft from which weapons could be fired (Fig. 3). (The word fo'c'sle still in use today is derived from this early construction.) Contemporary illustrations show that the castles resembled architectural forms with pillars, arches, and crenelations. They often were ornamented with carved and painted heraldic decorations with depictions of saints and animals, and with banners and flags flying from the masts indicating owners and national origins.

During and following the Middle Ages ships underwent many changes. For one, they became bigger. Decks and forecastles were enclosed, and masts were added to support additional sails. Some vessels had a bowsprit projecting from the bow under the overhanging forecastle, often with a carved animal head at the end of it. This type of ship was known as a carrack (Fig. 4).

The forward projecting superstructure of the carrack was enlarged to a degree that eventually impeded the ship's maneuverability. The high forecastle acted as a rigid sail, catching the wind and making it difficult to maintain a course. The English admiral Sir John Hawkins in 1570 is credited with designing a smaller, cut-back version of the forecastle, thus making ships more seaworthy and altering the profile of the bow.

European vessels adapted features from Mediterranean galleys. These multi-oared vessels usually had a small, raised forecastle to support weapons and below that a low horizontal platform called a beak. It projected forward and was used for ramming or boarding other vessels. The galley beak was added to carracks and was often elaborately carved. The horizontal beak below the reduced forecastle structure was known as a galleon-head.

3. Mediterranean sailing vessel of the 15th century with fore and aft "castles." Pl. CCCCXLVI from Creuze, *Treatise on the Theory and Practice of Naval Architecture* (Edinburgh, 1841).

The earliest known existing plans for English vessels are attributed to shipwright Matthew Baker (1530–1613) and are dated 1586. They show some figureheads mounted on the beaks of galleon-head warships (Fig. 5). At this time lions as a royal symbol were often used as figurehead subjects, not only on English ships but also in the Dutch and French navies. Due to the position of the beak, the lion figureheads were in a nearly horizontal, running position. The lions were often gilded, but when that was too expensive they were painted yellow or red.

Up to the mid-sixteenth century records of shipbuilding and shipcarvers are scarce. However, from then on there exist artists' sketchbooks, scale drawings, models, and naval records. The shape of the ship and its decoration was influenced by artistic considerations as well as by a growing scientific approach to shipbuilding.

One trend in ship design which the new scientific approach brought was the upward turn of the beak. The horizontal galleon-head, borrowed as it was from rowing craft, was ill-suited to the rough seas of the Atlantic. In the early seventeenth century the beak and supporting side rails were raised, at first at an angle and later in an upward convex curve.

4. Model of late 16th-century Spanish armed carrack *Madre de Dios*; model by Frederick Stern (d. 1961). L. 53 in. (134.6 cm.). Mystic Seaport Museum. Source: Mrs. Helen Smith, Robert A. Stern, Dr. Siegfried Stern, 62.237.

The first rate ship H.M.S. *Sovereign of the Seas*, built in 1637, is an example of the height of European ship decoration reached in the seventeenth century (Fig. 6). The slight upward slant of the bow was an indication of the changes to come. Although warship bows were to continue to change, the profusion of ornamentation lasted throughout the century. The former lion passant figureheads began to rear upright, at times leaning slightly backward as the curve of the bow structure increased. Human figures, sometimes in groups as on the bow of the *Sovereign of the Seas*, representing mythical and allegorical characters began to replace lions and leopards. The ship of the seventeenth century was a sculptural form, a riot of extraneous decoration.

At this time shipcarving was considered a fine art, and numerous drawings and sketchbooks of the period survive today indicating that it was an important occupation equal to that of the architect and sculptor. Carvers were employed in dockyards as well as palaces. Louis XIV's minister of naval affairs, Jean Baptiste Colbert (1619–1683), embarked on a project to make France's navy supreme on the seas. He hired sculptors to design and carve ship decorations that would reflect the grandeur of the Sun King. He organized dockyard schools for shipcarvers. Finally, ship decorations became too grandiose even for Colbert, and in 1674 he issued orders restricting shipcarving.

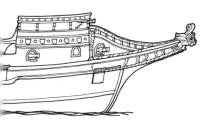

5. Galleon-head, after plan probably by British shipwright Matthew Baker, 1586, in the Pepysian Library, Cambridge, England. Drawn by Bill Gill.

6. British ship *Sovereign of the Seas* of 1637 with baroque profusion of ornament. Pl. ccccxlix from Creuze, *Treatise on the Theory and Practice of Naval Architecture* (Edinburgh, 1841).

While the shipcarvers were giving their talents free rein, the seamen found the encumbered vessels unmanageable, a situation reminiscent of the top-heavy carracks. There are accounts of crews covering figureheads with cages so that lines would not become fouled in the ornate protuberances.[3] There are stories of frustrated captains, once at sea, ordering applied ornaments cut off.

Beginning in the early seventeenth century armed merchant vessels were built by the East India companies. The East Indiamen (Fig. 7) were as richly ornamented as the warships of the royal navies, and they dominated European shipping for the next two hundred years. Some were built in British dockyards established in India. By the early nineteenth century these companies had lost their monopolies of trade in India and competition was open to private companies. As speed and capacity became important considerations these vessels shed much of their applied ornamentation and became more streamlined, but the figurehead remained.

7. Unidentified British East Indiaman at Calcutta, dated 1794, oil painting by Frans Balthazar Solvyns, Belgian (1760–1824). 26 1/2 x 47 7/8 in. (67.3 x 121.5 cm.). Peabody Museum of Salem, Massachusetts.

In 1716 the Admiralty issued an order requiring that a model be submitted for approval for every naval vessel built or rebuilt. Much of our knowledge about figureheads is obtained from these models, which were meticulous scale renderings of the actual vessels. The model of the H.M.S. *Burford* of 1722, which is in the Seaport's collection, is a splendid example. It shows in detail the upright lion rampant on the head as it had developed by that time (Fig. 9).

Throughout the eighteenth century in England, the Admiralty issued orders and counter orders regulating the style and cost of ship decoration. In spite of these regulations, which were often not obeyed, the design of ships and the profusion of carving remained relatively constant. There appears to have

8. Wash drawing of straddle figurehead for an unidentified vessel, by Yves Etienne Collet *aîné*, French (1761–1843). 18 3/4 x 24 3/4 in. (47.6 x 62.9 cm.). Mystic Seaport Museum. Source: Richard S. Perkins, 60.290.

been a continual struggle during this time between artists inclined toward massive ship decoration, which was encouraged by the monarchs' desire for display, and the shipbuilders' practical approach to ship design. It was only by the end of the century that ornamentation declined significantly.

In 1703 the Admiralty limited bow decoration to a lion and trailboards. In 1727 that order was revoked, and figureheads other than lions were permitted, especially on smaller vessels. In 1742 a regulation raised the heads and rails, thus changing the shape of the bow. In 1773 an order regulated the amount of money allowed for shipcarving. Another order in 1796 limited bow decoration to billetheads. Although this ruling was not popular, it was at this time that small bust figureheads began to appear on frigates and smaller vessels.[4]

The sketches of Yves Etienne Collet *aîné* (1761–1843) in the Seaport's collection depict French figureheads in the style of the late eighteenth century. One drawing (Fig. 8) depicts a classical warrior mounted astraddle the cutwater. The figurehead is still ornate, but is subdued compared to those of the previous century.

9. Straddle figurehead of rampant lion on bow of British Admiralty model of H.M.S. *Burford*, 1722. L. overall 60 in. (152.4 cm.). Mystic Seaport Museum. Source: John P. Morgan II, in honor of his father, Junius S. Morgan, 73.147.

Developments in the United States

On the western side of the Atlantic, shipbuilding and shipcarving in colonial America closely followed English examples on a modest scale. Ship carpenters and carvers came to the colonies, and their services were readily employed. Upon arrival they set up shops and advertised themselves as artists, carvers, or artists in wood. They often emphasized their previous apprenticeships and experience.

M. V. Brewington in *Shipcarvers of North America* writes in detail about the development of the shipcarver's trade. He notes that the earliest known definite mention of an American figurehead is from the bill of carvers Edward Budd and Richard Knight of Boston. This bill is for a lion on the sloop *Speedwell* of 1689. Between the time of that bill and the signing of the Declaration of Independence, shipcarvers' shops proliferated in such major shipbuilding centers as Boston, New York, and Philadelphia, as well as in smaller coastal towns.

In 1775 the Continental Congress ordered that thirteen frigates be built, with designs approved by the Marine Commission and carving decisions left to the individual shipwrights. Two of these frigates are known to have had full-length portrait figureheads representing the men for whom the ships were named, Sir Walter Raleigh and John Hancock. A third frigate, the *Boston*, carried a full-length figure of an American Indian, a subject that recurred on the bows of American vessels in the nineteenth century.

As the nation grew and prospered, the United States took the lead in the design of a new type of ship. The highest achievement of the wooden shipbuilder's art arrived in the 1840s with the clipper ship. Built for speed rather than capacity, the elegant clippers would not accommodate superfluous weight. On many, however, the figurehead survived as the center of attention on the prow. With the clipper ship a further transformation of the bow occurred. The last remnants of the forward convex stem and protruding front structure vanished. The cutwater of the clipper was concave, and the figurehead, formerly upright, stretched forward at an angle as though reaching out (Fig. 10). Clipper ship figureheads usually represented people, sometimes allegorical, but often the person for whom the vessel was named. Two other popular subjects were the American Indian and the bald eagle, both symbols of the new nation.

The American whaleship, a rugged peasant compared to the aristocratic clipper, often carried a billethead or bust figure on its bow (Fig. 11). Many whaleship owners and captains, especially those in New Bedford and Nantucket, were Quakers who took a dim view of personal adornment. There is an account of a mock funeral in 1785 for the figurehead from the New Bedford whaleship *Rebecca*. The figure, which was a carving of a woman, was thought by the owners to be inappropriate.[5]

Figureheads on whalers often represented members of the captain's or owner's family. They vary greatly in quality: some were obviously carved by trained artists and others in workmanship and style are more akin to folk art.

Small figureheads and billetheads also adorned the bows of schooners of the period, and there is a tradition of figureheads on yachts as well.

Unlike the European artist under royal patronage, the American shipcarver was self-employed, usually hired by the shipowner rather than by the builder. Thus, figureheads were sometimes carved in one town and the ship built in another. On occasion this arrangement necessitated frequent communication between the carver, builder, and owner in order to determine correct sizes, proportions, and details. For example, on 6 March 1850, the Boston carvers S. W. Gleason & Sons wrote to the Portsmouth, New Hampshire, shipbuilders Fernald & Pettigrew concerning the figurehead of the ship *Western World*:

> Your favor of the 5th inst is at hand together with the sketch of the head of the *Western World*, for which we are greatly obliged to you & which no doubt will be of some assistance to us in regard to thickness of cut water &c &c. You have sent us the rake of the stem & steve of bowsprit: if you will please let us know about the distance you want the upper-side of lower cheek from the underside of the bowsprit on the line of the stem, & the distance you want the figure to set out on the line of the bowsprit, and the distance out on the bowsprit of the inner bobstay, we shall be able to furnish a draft on a scale to set the head by: or perhaps it would be better if you would lay the model on a sheet of paper & mark the line of the stem & the shear of the wale streak, this is necessary as the butt end of the lower-cheek should start on a parallel line, . . .[6]

The letter goes on to give proposed dimensions of the figurehead, apparently to be a full-length female figure, and specifications for stern carving. It ends by stating, "We have no doubt that you can have the figure before the first of July."[7]

Brewington lists nearly two hundred shipcarvers working in the United States in the nineteenth century. William Rush (1756–1833) of Philadelphia, considered the United States' first major shipcarver, is credited with introducing the striding figure to American vessels. He was the son of a shipwright and was apprenticed to a shipcarver before becoming one of the foremost artists of his time. The Salem, Massachusetts, furniture maker Samuel McIntire (1757–1811) also did some shipcarving. The Skillin family of Boston, Philadelphia, and New York had firmly established themselves before the Revolution. By mid-century the United States had scores of native shipcarvers who relied more on their own talents than on artistic influences from abroad. The shipcarving shops of the Gleasons in Boston and the Andersons in New York were flourishing, and there was enough demand for their work to support the scores of shipcarvers in smaller coastal towns.

10. Shortly after being launched at Mystic, Connecticut, in 1855, the medium clipper *Belle Hoxie* was sold and renamed *Andrew Jackson*; under the concave bow is the striding, full-length figurehead of her second namesake. Oil painting by unidentified artist. 31 3/8 x 43 7/16 in. (79.7 x 110.4 cm.). Mystic Seaport Museum. Source: Mrs. Richard D. Wilcox, 41.662.

11. American whaleship *Alexander*, built 1821, Chatham, Connecticut, carried an upright bust figurehead of a man. Watercolor by unidentified artist, ca. 1821. 15 1/2 x 20 in. (39.3 x 50.8 cm.). Peabody Museum of Salem, Massachusetts. Photograph: M.W. Sexton.

12. Flat lacing piece carved on back of Woman with Gold Belt; four drifts are still in place. Mystic Seaport Museum. Source: Harold H. Kynett, 53.3099.

Decline of Shipcarving

The nineteenth century saw the introduction of iron- and steel-built ships. Even more significant was the introduction of steam power. Eventually, these innovations altered radically and irreversibly the shape of ocean-going vessels. Ships no longer dependent on sails abandoned the bowsprit. The plumb stem was introduced, eliminating the natural place for the figurehead. However, design adaptations followed slowly behind the engineering advances, and the figurehead survived until there was literally no place for it. In 1894 the British Admiralty abolished the figurehead from major ships.[8] In 1909 the U. S. Secretary of the Navy ordered the removal of figureheads from all fighting vessels except the bronze one designed by Augustus Saint-Gaudens on Admiral Dewey's flagship *Olympia*.[9] Shipcarving, once a thriving business in coastal shipbuilding towns and cities, disappeared except for an occasional anachronistic revival. As the demand for shipcarving declined, carvers turned their skills more to other types of figures such as cigar store Indians and circus wagon figures.

The Making of the Figurehead

In the United States most figureheads were carved from white pine. This wood is soft and easily carved. In Europe the hardwoods oak and elm were commonly used. Figureheads were often carved from one piece of wood for durability and carved with the grain to reduce splintering. Many nineteenth-century figureheads of full-length women in classical robes are remarkably similar in pose and expression, which may mean that there were stock figures. Arms and other appendages not held close to the body were carved separately and notched and bolted to the figure. Laminating and piecing together wood pieces was avoided because of the chance of separation due to weathering. One notable exception to this is the *Great Republic* eagle (Fig. 24), which is made up of seven pieces of wood pieced together.

After being carved, the figurehead was covered with a coat of lead paint and then either gilded or painted in natural colors. The preservation of the figurehead depended upon the quality of the finish and its upkeep. Therefore, after a period of time at sea the figurehead was often painted over with additional coats of white lead paint. Contemporary paintings and photographs show figureheads painted both in colors and in monochrome.

Busts as well as full-length figures were carved in the round with a section on the back or base left flat or cut out. This area, known as a lacing piece (Fig. 12) butted against the stem of the vessel. Bolts (threaded) or drifts (metal rods) were then driven from the front of the figure, through the abutting vessel timber and fastened. Bungs (Fig. 13) covered the bolt holes on the front and were painted over. Often a bust figurehead had a mortise carved out in the base

(Fig. 14) to fit over a corresponding tenon on the top of the stem. Extended arms or in some instances the entire figurehead itself may have been removed and stowed below for protection from the beating of the waves.

Prices paid for carvings varied greatly from artist to artist and from one type of figurehead to another. A letter dated 14 September 1847 from Boston shipcarver J. W. Mason to shipbuilders Fernald & Pettigrew poignantly sheds light on an eternal problem.

> Your large Eagle is carved but not gilt and I want you to grant me a few days more to gild it in. I can get it well done by Saturday so that you can put it in on Monday — three days will not make any difference with you I hope. I have cheated myself in this job. I ought to have charged you $10 more — it will cost me more than I anticipated to gild it. He is a BOUNCER. Carvers get sheared sometimes as well as ship builders — It will all be the same a hundred years hence.[10]

The irony is, of course, that there were no shipcarvers a century later.

13. Woman with Binoculars; the bungs on the center of the skirt cover holes made by bolts driven through the figure into the abutting timber, also called a lacing piece, on the vessel. Mystic Seaport Museum. Source: Mrs. Harriet Greenman Stillman, 33.85.

14. Bust of a Man; the mortise in the base fit over a notch on the stem; the cross of the T rested on the upper ends of the lower cheek knees; see Fig. 22. Mystic Seaport Museum. Source: Weston Howland, 47.1177.

21

Chapter 2

The Growth of the Figurehead Collection

In December 1929, Edward E. Bradley, Carl C. Cutler, and Dr. Charles K. Stillman founded The Marine Historical Association, what is today Mystic Seaport Museum. Their purpose was to found an educational institution dedicated to preserving America's illustrious maritime past.[1] The immediate tasks confronting the three founders were to collect artifacts, to stimulate an interest in the Association, and to acquire proper building facilities to house the collection.[2] This was an enormous undertaking.

The first year the collection grew slowly, with only twenty-eight acquisitions consisting mostly of half models, logbooks, and library material. In the following year 219 items were accessioned, ranging from a sandbagger sloop, the first vessel in the collection, to oil paintings. It was not until 1933 that the museum acquired its first figurehead.

In 1933 Dr. Stillman's mother, Harriet Greenman Stillman, daughter of Mystic shipbuilder Clark Greenman, bought two figureheads from a Boston antique dealer and gave them to the Association. They were a bust carving of a man, known as "Asia" (Fig. 71), and a three-quarter-length figure of a woman holding binoculars (Figs. 54, 55). The following year Mrs. Stillman purchased for the museum the bust figure of "Orlando"(Fig. 75). By the end of the decade, with two more contributions from the Stillmans, one from an anonymous donor, and one Association purchase, the number of figureheads had increased to seven. This was the beginning of the collection, which over the next thirty years grew to include nearly seventy figureheads.

In 1934 the Seaport's first exhibit was opened to the public for two afternoons a week during July and August, in the converted machine shop of the old Mystic Manufacturing Co., now known as the Wendell Building.[3] By the summer of 1936 the exhibit days were increased to three afternoons a week, but still only during July and August. *The New London Day* ran an article on 18 July 1936, called "Rare Marine Curios Displayed at Mystic Museum," and accompanying the article were photographs of the exhibit in which "Asia" and "Orlando" were featured as prominent attractions.[4]

In 1938 two of the three founders of The Marine Historical Association, Edward Bradley and Charles K. Stillman, died, leaving Carl Cutler as Managing Director of the Association. It was he who, with the encouragement and financial support of Board of Trustees President Clifford Day Mallory, Sr., began an active search for figureheads.

Figureheads, salvaged shipwreck victims, were often left outside, neglected and subject to decay. As a historian Cutler knew that in time few of these relics would remain. As an administrator he knew that a figurehead collection could spark the interest of the visiting public and attract potential donors. In December 1938, he wrote to Mallory expressing his aim in collecting figureheads:

> My interest in them has been aroused mainly by the fact that people seem to regard them as the principal criterion by which they judge a museum - as witness the Mariner's Museum. I am not at all sure a smashing good collection would not be, on the whole, the most inexpensive way of kindling the enthusiasm of such people as Mrs. Harkness to the point that they will voluntarily ask to co-operate.[5]

The same winter, in February 1939, he wrote to a friend in New York telling him of the favorable progress the Museum had made in recent months and explaining what was still needed:

> We need, especially, to get more of such things as figure heads, and other old relics from ships - steering wheels, binnacles, name boards, etc. Now it seems to me that it is quite likely that down around Newfoundland and the French Islands there must be a lot of such things from wrecked ships. Do you think of any of your connections down there who would be willing to look up some of the stuff and buy it and ship it to us? . . . Mallory is very keen on it and he has told me to go ahead and he will see that the money is there when needed. He has gone ahead on his own account and asked some connections in Scotland to get all such material they can and ship it along.[6]

Thus began the search for figureheads. The quest extended from the Cape Verde Islands to the Northwest Coast, from Scotland to Australia, any place where there might be stranded or derelict ships with bows intact. Cutler wrote to his wide range of friends and colleagues asking them to be on the lookout for figureheads for the museum. During the early years of The Marine Historical Association, collecting was almost indiscriminate, with little regard for the age, condition, or national origin of artifacts, as long as they had marine associations. Later a more methodical approach took over, and the Museum developed a refined collections policy.

16. Carved eagle from four-masted bark *Great Republic* at the door of the Public Library in Stonington, Connecticut. Photographed by Thomas Whitridge Cutler, before 1928. Photograph: Mystic Seaport Museum, 50.910.

By the end of the 1940s the number of figureheads in the Seaport's collection had grown to twenty-three. The dramatic growth was due to several factors. First of all, the active search begun in the 1930s continued. Also, the museum had grown in size and prestige, which attracted donors and lenders to the collection. Finally, appearing on the scene at this time was a benefactor who was to become instrumental in the growth of the figurehead collection. This was Philadelphia businessman Harold H. Kynett.

During his thirty-two years as trustee, from 1941 until his death in 1973, H. H. Kynett contributed the funds to purchase and ship to Mystic nearly half of what is the present figurehead collection. Over the years he became increasingly interested in acquiring figureheads for the Kynett Collection at the museum. His financial generosity and Cutler's ceaseless inquiries contributed to finding and acquiring many of these carvings. On 13 December 1948, Kynett wrote to Cutler that "my own inclination is to put every penny that I can spare into figureheads when we can get them."[7]

In 1947, Thomas A. Stevens replaced Carl Cutler as Managing Director, and Cutler, in addition to his continued responsibilities as Secretary, was appointed Curator. This reorganization relieved him of administrative duties and left him more time for collections work.

25

Close to home was the dramatic eagle figurehead from the four-masted bark *Great Republic* (see Fig. 24), which had been for many years on exhibit in Stonington, Connecticut, at the Public Library and later at the Lighthouse Museum (Fig. 16). This figurehead was owned by the descendants of Captain Nathaniel B. Palmer of Stonington, who had acquired it at the time he was involved with the rebuilding of the ship after she burned to the water in 1853 shortly after her launching. The owners decided to transfer the figurehead loan from the Lighthouse Museum to Mystic Seaport, where it would be seen by more people. This was the first positively identified and authenticated figurehead acquired by the Museum. The eagle was on loan for twenty-eight years until 1976 when it was purchased by Mystic Seaport from the Palmer heirs.

Sometimes the pursuit of a figurehead took years. Such was the case with the figurehead from the Black Ball packet ship *Donald McKay* (Fig. 25). For many years Cutler had known that this figurehead, detached from its ship, was on the Cape Verde Island of St. Vincent (Fig. 15). The ship had ended her days under German registry as a coal hulk in the Madeira Islands.[8] Alain Gerbault in his book *In Quest of the Sun* reported seeing the carving in 1929 on a stopover at St. Vincent.[9] Through correspondence and coincidence the owner of the carving and the Museum became known to each other, and in July 1949 the Museum received a letter from Ricardo Pinto Serradas of St. Vincent.

> Dear Sirs, I have been informed that sometime ago you showed interest in obtaining the "DONALD MC.KAY" figurehead . . . I have pleasure in informing you that the figurehead in question is in my possession . . . I should, therefore, be glad to hear from you whether you are still interested in the figurehead and how you are prepared to obtain same.[10]

The transatlantic negotiations which ensued resulted in the Seaport's purchasing the figurehead from Serradas and shipping it to Mystic with funds provided by Kynett. Upon its arrival at the Museum what photographs had shown was all too apparent. The once magnificent figure was badly weathered from years of exposure and neglect, and much restoration was needed before placing it on exhibit.

By the end of the 1940s the figureheads had become an important area of the Museum's collection. In October 1948, the Museum opened a special exhibition of figureheads. In addition to the carvings already in the collection, this exhibit included six on loan from the Sewall Collection of Bath, Maine, and four new acquisitions by Kynett.[11]

By this time, too, the operations of the Museum were running smoothly, and in the winter of 1949–1950 Cutler was granted a three-month leave of absence to rest and write. For a change of scene and in order to escape daily interruptions he decided to spend his sabbatical in Vancouver, British Columbia. Having lived there as a young man the area was familiar and

17. Carl C. Cutler, curator of the Marine Historical Association, with the figurehead from the bark *Balasore* at Redonda Island, British Columbia, 7 March 1950; a few days later the figurehead was crated and shipped by train to Mystic.

26

agreeable to him.[12] It was also a region known to have been the last stop for some large vessels that in their prime bore figureheads. Shortly before his departure for the northwest, Cutler wrote to Kynett telling of his hope of finding more figureheads:

> The Tusler letter suggests to my optimistic soul the possibility of digging up several figureheads on the West Coast, a thing I have tried to do by correspondence for seven long years. Accordingly, if I do go to the Coast, it may cost you plenty. I would expect, however, to get figureheads there - if available at all - for around half the cost here.[13]

As far as figureheads were concerned, Cutler's sojourn in Vancouver was both frustrating and exciting. He found himself engaged in lengthy correspondence and arduous trips by train, truck, and boat to back-country logging camps. (By this time, Cutler was an energetic seventy-one years old.) The lumber industry in the area made use of old sailing ships that had outlived their usefulness on the open seas and converted them to lumber barges. One company engaged in this work was the Powell River Company of Vancouver. They had used the four-masted steel bark *Balasore* for such purposes. Her figurehead still existed (Fig. 37), although it had long since been separated from the vessel (Fig. 17). The Powell River Co. agreed to donate the carving if the Museum would pay for transporting it East.[14] This the Museum was able to do thanks to H. H. Kynett.

Keeping his benefactor informed of progress, Cutler wrote to Kynett several days before returning to Mystic, in March of 1950:

> My head is bloody and still bowed. The West Coast trip rated a goose egg. Barker [a carpenter and guide] said that the heavy storms had washed in the sand and covered up the wrecks almost completely. Aside from that he found an old beachcomber who said he had two figureheads that he had rolled up on the beach. He took Barker on an eight mile jaunt and then couldn't find them - said the sand must have blown over them.
>
> . . . I got the figurehead [from *Balasore*] and have had it crated and cleared for shipment via Seattle. We had a three day trip but no trouble except that some fool had set the figure a foot deep in concrete and it took four hours to dig it out. It is just a little under 8 feet tall and took seven men to carry it, and they rested every fifty feet. It is in very good shape, except for a little rot where it set in the concrete.[15]

18. South wing of Stillman Building as it looked from 1958 to 1975.
Photographed in 1967.

19 (opposite). Spotlighted figureheads on exhibit in the Wendell Building, since 1975.
Photographed in 1977.

Shortly after the arrival of the *Balasore* figurehead from Vancouver in the spring of 1950, the Kynett Collection was formally installed in the south end of the Wendell Building. Included in the exhibit in addition to paintings, prints, and models were twelve figureheads.[16] However, by 1952 the Kynett Collection had outgrown the space and was moved to the roomier second floor of the Stillman Building. The Wendell Building was then able to accommodate, among other exhibits, objects recently acquired from the Tarkington estate.[17]

For several years Cutler had corresponded with the novelist and play-wright Booth Tarkington, mostly about the possibility of salvaging Tarkington's schooner *Regina* in Kennebunkport, Maine. In 1946 Tarkington died, and in the years following the *Regina* deteriorated beyond repair. In 1952 Cutler resumed his interest in the collection and this time corresponded with the author's secretary, Miss Elizabeth Trotter. They agreed that part of the collection, including two figureheads (Figs. 51, 52), should come to Mystic as a memorial to Tarkington.

Tarkington did not consider himself a collector, but acquired maritime artifacts because he liked them or was given them.[18] Unlike many of the figureheads in the Museum's collection, the two from the Tarkington estate had not been restored, although originally the bust figure had probably been cut down from full length. In their natural but weathered state they have nonetheless escaped the alterations of repair.

Also in 1952 the building then known as the Colgrove Memorial was built on the Seaport grounds to provide exhibit space for the modelmaker's and shipcarver's shops.[19] This building with a shipcarver's exhibit was opened to the public in 1963.[20]

In the 1950s thirty-nine more figureheads were added to the collection. Important additions were a large carving from the *Magdalena* (Fig. 35), a portrait bust of a woman that was identified twenty-five years later as being from the brig *Eunice H. Adams* (Fig. 20), an Indian figure from the ship *Seminole* (Fig. 27), and the figure of Admiral David Glasgow Farragut from the ship *Great Admiral* (Fig. 28).

In 1958 the Museum acquired by a Kynett purchase from the Port Adelaide (Australia) Nautical Museum the figurehead from the Mystic-built ship *Seminole*. Because of the figurehead's local origins the Museum was particularly interested in obtaining this striding figure. In 1957 Edouard A. Stackpole, then Curator, wrote to the Australian museum to ask if the Seaport could purchase the carving.[21] The figurehead had been in Australia since the turn of the century when the vessel was converted for use as a storeship in Adelaide.[22] It was an important piece to the Port Adelaide Museum, as well, but reluctantly they agreed to part with it. At a dedication of the figurehead at the Seaport in the summer of 1958, Jeremiah Holmes, the eighty-five-year-old grandnephew of *Seminole*'s captain J. Warren Holmes of Mystic, was present.[23]

In 1958 the figurehead collection was again rehung, this time high on the walls in the south wing of the Stillman Building (Fig. 18).[24] There the carvings remained for nearly twenty years until 1977 when the figurehead exhibit was opened in the Wendell Building (Fig. 19). For the first time in the history of the Seaport an exhibit was assembled exclusively devoted to figureheads. Unlike the arrangement characteristic of earlier Museum exhibits, this one displayed the figureheads in simplicity and grandeur.

After the 1950s only four figureheads, all from unidentified vessels, were acquired. The last figurehead received by the Seaport was the figure of an eagle from an unknown vessel, donated by the estate of George B. Mitchell in 1967.

After fifty years of collecting there is no longer a rush to build the collection. Efforts are now directed toward refining and preserving the collection as well as acquiring the truly exceptional figurehead in good condition. There are also not as many carvings available. Many have been absorbed by museums and private collections, and many others have disintegrated. The lack of documented provenance further reduces the number of desirable figureheads.

Chapter 3

The Collection:
Identified Figureheads

Nineteenth-century figureheads differed in size, subject, and style as the ships that bore them varied in design, rig, and use. Categorizing the Seaport's identified figureheads according to vessel types groups the carvings in a roughly chronological order. Comparisons of these known figureheads to similar, but unidentified ones in the collection help to date and determine the origin of the unidentified carvings (see chapter 4).

Most of the figureheads in the Museum are of unknown or uncertain origin. Of the nearly seventy in the collection, only twelve can be positively attributed to identified vessels, of which seven were built in the United States and five in Europe.

Small Merchant Vessels and Whalers

It is not surprising that with one exception all of the Seaport's American figureheads are from well-known ships. The one exception is a bust carving from the schooner, later brig, *Eunice H. Adams* (Fig. 20). When this figurehead was given to the Museum in 1956 its identity was a mystery, but as a result of research twenty-five years later the vessel's name has been discovered. This figurehead is the earliest dated one in the collection.

20. Bust figurehead from American schooner, later brig, *Eunice H. Adams*, built Bristol, Rhode Island, 1845, by Amos Crandall. White pine. H. 17 3/4 in. (45.1 cm.). Source: Charles Francis Adams, Jr., Mrs. Henry S. Morgan, 56.745.

A staff researcher[1] noticed the unmistakable resemblance between the Seaport's figurehead and a sternboard portrait from the *Eunice H. Adams* in the Whaling Museum, New Bedford, Massachusetts (Fig. 21). A search for pictures of the vessel unearthed a photograph of her with the figurehead clearly visible (Fig. 22). Comparison of identical wood cracks visible in the photograph of the figurehead and on the Seaport's bust positively identified the carving as being the same one shown in the photograph.

21. Fragment of a painted pine sternboard from the *Eunice H. Adams*, portraying Mrs. Adams with a book. 17 1/2 x 91 1/2 in. (44.5 x 231.7 cm.). The Whaling Museum, New Bedford, Massachusetts.

The *Bristol Phenix* of 11 October 1845 noted the launching the previous Saturday of the eighty-two-foot, 118-ton schooner from the Bristol, Rhode Island, shipyard of Amos Crandall. According to the short article, she was a fine vessel:

> This, we think is one of the best and most substantial vessels ever built in this State. Her timbers are of white oak, and as large as those of a ship of three hundred tons. She is copper fastened throughout, well finished, and will undoubtedly be a fast sailer as well as a great carrier. Crandall's vessels are acknowledged on all hands to be equal to any built in New England.[2]

Eunice H. Adams sailed for more than half a century. She was named for the wife of Freeman E. Adams, one of the owners, of Nantucket. She began her career carrying cargo between Nantucket and Baltimore.[3] In 1867 she was rerigged as a hermaphrodite brig and in 1869 was sold by Adams to New Bedford, from whence she made many whaling voyages in the Atlantic.[4] She does not appear in ship registers after 1898, and we may assume that she was broken up for scrap and her figurehead removed around that time.

Sometime before 1902 Henry M. Plummer of New Bedford bought the figurehead and gave it to Charles Francis Adams II of Boston.[5] The figurehead was given to the Seaport by Charles Francis Adams, Jr., and his sister, Mrs. Henry S. Morgan.

Eunice Hopkins Nickerson [Adams] was born in Cotuit, Massachusetts, on 12 November 1811, and married Freeman E. Adams on 9 March 1835.[6] Freeman and his brother, Zenas L. Adams, owned and operated craft ranging from schooners to catboats from Steamboat (New North) Wharf in Nantucket. Freeman died in 1876 at the age of sixty-four,[7] and his wife died on 23 September 1900, at the age of eighty-eight.[8]

According to a newspaper article in *The New Bedford Evening Standard* of 1902, although the *Eunice H. Adams* was named for the owner's wife, the figurehead was actually modeled after Mrs. Adams's sister.[9] Ship registers of New Bedford show that several vessels were owned jointly by Freeman and members of Mrs. Adams's family and her in-laws, indicating that the families were closely associated.[10]

The bust portrait has an individual quality about it, and it is undoubtedly a good likeness of the person who posed for it. Although the artist is not known, the figurehead was obviously made by a skilled carver. The difference in style and expression between it and the sternboard portrait may be due to possible restoration of the sternboard (there has been no restoration of the figurehead at the Seaport). Another possibility is that the two carvings may have been made by different artists working in the same shop, not an uncommon practice in the apprentice tradition of the nineteenth-century woodcarver's trade.[11]

On the vessel itself, carved trailboards extended from the base of the figurehead aft to the hawsehole. The figurehead was mortised at a slight forward angle atop the stempost, with the lacing piece on back of the bust butting flush against the bow. There is a bolt just below the brooch on the bodice that went through the figurehead, securing it to the bow of the vessel. The entire figurehead, including the lacing piece, is carved from a single piece of white pine with the grain running vertically.[12]

22. Bow of brig *Eunice H. Adams* with figurehead in place. Probably photographed in New Bedford in the late 1890s at the end of her career. Photograph: The Whaling Museum, New Bedford, Massachusetts.

Two unidentified figureheads in the collection bear a remarkable similarity to the *Eunice H. Adams* carving, and it is possible that they were carved for the same type of vessel around the same time. One in particular, a small bust of a woman (Fig. 48) may have been made by the same carver. The size, hair style, dress, collar, encircling drapery, and absence of front billet scroll are all features that resemble those on the *Eunice H. Adams* figurehead. The delicate, individualized features suggest that it, too, was an actual portrait.

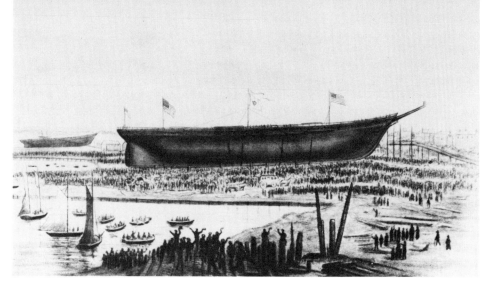

23. At the time of her launching at Donald McKay's East Boston shipyard in 1853, the *Great Republic* was the largest American-built merchant sailing ship. From McKay, *Some Famous Sailing Ships and Their Builder, Donald McKay* (New York, 1928), opp. p. 230.

The other figurehead resembling these two is a bust carving of a man (Fig. 50). It is similar in size to the two female busts and also lacks the billet scroll in front that was so often an element used at the base of small bust figureheads. Similar, too, are the carved rosettes in the centers of the side scrolls which are common to all three.

That all three busts came to the Museum from donors living in New England indicates that the two unidentified ones also may be originally from New England vessels, probably ones much like the *Eunice H. Adams*. Small personalized figureheads such as these reflected the owners' pride in their ships, occupations, and families.

Ships and Clipper Ships

In the mid-1840s at the same time whalers and small merchant vessels like the *Eunice H. Adams* were being launched, American shipbuilders were developing a new type of ship. The discovery of gold in California and Australia and increased trade with the Far East created an economic need for faster ships that could shorten the sailing time around the Cape of Good Hope and Cape Horn. For this trade shipbuilders created light and swift clipper ships, with their new concave bows and tall rigs made for speed. They were often named for their owners and builders, and many carried large, full-length figureheads of their namesakes or of national symbols. Today not a single intact American clipper ship survives, but some of their figureheads have been preserved.

The foremost American shipbuilder of the middle of the nineteenth century was Donald McKay. Among the many ships launched from his East Boston shipyard was the four-masted bark *Great Republic*. Designed and built in 1853 by McKay on speculation for his own account, this was the largest ship built in the United States up to that time, and it promised to be the fastest and most profitable. A public holiday was declared in Boston on 4 October 1853 for her launching,[13] and the event is said to have been attended by fifty thousand people (Fig. 23).[14]

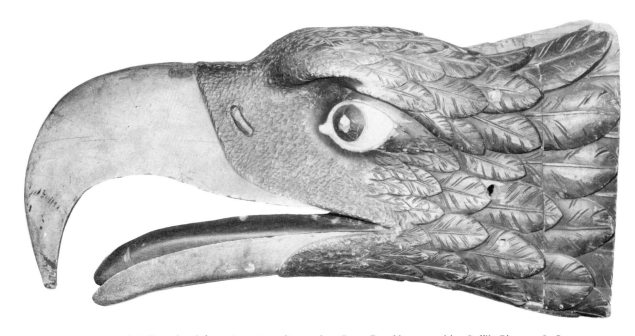

24. Figurehead from American clipper ship *Great Republic*, carved by S. W. Gleason & Sons, Boston. The abruptly cut end of the neck indicates that there may have been some additional carving that did not survive the December 1853 fire. White pine. L. 61 in. (154.9 cm.). Source: Museum purchase, 48.942.

The figurehead of this ship was a splendid carved head of a bald eagle (Fig. 24). Austere in its simplicity, the eagle head was a departure from the frequently used full-length or bust figures of people. One contemporary account suggests that the carving was not well received:

> The angular form of her bow, however, is preserved entire; and such a bow for sharpness, beauty and strength, has never before been produced in this country. Yet it is plain, even to nakedness, having the national eagle represented as emerging from below the bowsprit, as its only ornament. But even simple and appropriate as is this ornament, it adds nothing to the beauty of the bow.[15]

This same source later adds: "Messrs. Gleason & Co. ornamented her head and stern."[16] Carvers of numerous figureheads for clipper ships, the firm of S. W. Gleason & Sons was active in Boston from 1847 until 1854. After that the firm underwent changes in partnership, continuing in business under different names until 1896.[17]

After her launching the *Great Republic* sailed to New York City, where she was to be loaded with cargo for her maiden voyage to Liverpool under the command of Lauchlan McKay, brother of the builder. On the day after Christmas 1853, fire broke out at the Novelty Baking Co. on Front Street and spread to the wharf where the *Great Republic* was berthed. The new ship caught fire and burned to the waterline.

36

McKay gave the vessel up to the insurance underwriters, and she was later sold to A. A. Low & Brother of New York. The ship was rebuilt and considerably altered from her original design by Sneeden & Whitlock at Greenpoint, Brooklyn, under the supervision of Captain Nathaniel Brown Palmer (1799–1877).[18] In place of the eagle, the rebuilt *Great Republic* had a carved billethead.[19]

In his youth Captain Palmer had commanded the sloop *Hero* in 1820–1821 on a sealing voyage that was one of the earliest voyages made to the Antarctic archipelago. It was presumably Palmer who had the *Great Republic*'s figurehead removed, and it descended to his heirs in Stonington, Connecticut, who, in 1948, presented it to the Museum on loan. In 1976 the Museum purchased it from them.

The *Great Republic*'s eagle is carved of white pine[20] and is made up of seven pieces of wood. There is a vertical slit varying in width from 2¾ to 3½ inches through the center of the neck, which once fit over the narrow edge of the stem of the vessel. Remains of the copper fastenings used to secure the head to the bow still exist. Some evidence from contemporary illustrations indicates that the figurehead was originally longer, with additional neck feathers extending down the cutwater for several feet. Although no contemporary close-up photographs have come to light, schematic drawings made at the time of her launching show that the neck was longer. Remarkably, there are no signs of fire damage on the head, and it is possible that the lower neck was burned and sawed off. The eagle's open mouth was apparently hollowed out with an auger, as there are traces of the spiral gouge marks made by that tool. Today the figurehead is painted brown, and it is difficult to tell how it was painted at her launching. Contemporary prints and paintings show it a light color, which may mean it was painted white or gilded, either of which would have been appropriate. In nature, of course, the bald eagle's head and upper neck feathers are white.[21]

While the *Great Republic* was being rebuilt in New York, Donald McKay was at work in Boston designing a new ship. Under contract for the Liverpool shipowner James Baines (1823–1899), McKay was building another clipper, the *Donald McKay*, to join the British Black Ball fleet of Liverpool-to-Australia packets. In 1853 Baines had ordered four vessels from the Boston yard: *Lightning, Champion of the Seas, James Baines,* and *Donald McKay,* the last one named in honor of the builder Baines so admired. The *McKay* was launched in January 1855, and had a figurehead of a Scotsman wearing the McKay tartan (Fig. 25).

25. Figurehead from American clipper ship *Donald McKay*, launched 1855, East Boston. The figure has been restored and repainted after years of wear standing outside. H. 96 in. (243.2 cm.).
Source: Harold H. Kynett, 49.1414.

This figurehead may have been made in the United States, in England, or even at sea. It is known that the Gleasons carved several figureheads for McKay, including the eagle for the *Great Republic*. It is also known that Baines himself posed for William Dodd of Liverpool, who carved the figurehead for the *James Baines*. In an interview in later life Dodd is quoted as saying,

> The figurehead of the Donald MacKay, which, of course, was a rough likeness of that celebrated shipbuilder himself, was lost at sea. It was replaced by one made by the carpenter on board, and he made a pretty fair job of it.[22]

If this story is true, it is possible that the Seaport's figurehead is the one carved on shipboard.

The figurehead has undergone extensive restoration at the Museum to repair rot and damage. For many years before being acquired by the Seaport in 1949 it had stood outside, exposed and unprotected, on St. Vincent Island (Fig. 15).

A decade after the launching of the *Donald McKay*, at the end of the clipper era, the medium clipper *Seminole* was built in 1865 in Mystic, Connecticut, at the Maxson & Fish yard located a mile downriver from the site of Mystic Seaport Museum. This ship was built for Lawrence Giles & Co. of New York for the California trade (Fig. 26).

26 (opposite). American clipper ship *Seminole*, designed and built in Mystic, Connecticut, by Maxson & Fish, 1865. She is shown here at San Francisco, one of her frequent ports of call. Photograph: Mystic Seaport Museum, 39.2179.

27. Figurehead attributed to carvers Campbell & Colby, from Mystic-built merchant ship *Seminole* of 1865. H. 76. in. (193 cm.). Source: Harold H. Kynett, 58.632.

Named for the Florida tribe, the ship carried a figurehead of a full-length American Indian (Fig. 27). The carving represents the nineteenth-century stereotyped vision of an Indian. The clothing and decorations are not specifically those of the Seminoles, but rather represent the nineteenth-century idea of what an American Indian looked like.[23]

The Indian was often romanticized in American folklore, glorified in paintings and literature. He was an element uniquely American and as such was a powerful symbol for the United States. Representing courage and strength, he was an appropriate and frequently used subject for figureheads on American vessels; for example, American wood carver William Rush (1756–1833) probably designed and carved four Indian figureheads between 1789 and 1824.[24]

It is quite possible that the *Seminole* figurehead was carved by the Mystic firm of Campbell & Colby. Although no specific documentation has been found to confirm this attribution, John Newton Colby (ca. 1833–1891) and James Campbell (1834–1906) were active in Mystic from ca. 1859 to 1877.[25] To date they are the only carvers known to have had a shop in Mystic. They are known to have made decorations for ships besides doing non-marine work including sign carving and gilding. During this period Mystic was a prosperous shipbuilding center with seven major shipyards on the Mystic River and numerous smaller boatyards in the area between Noank and Old Mystic.

28 (opposite). Portrait figurehead of naval hero David Glasgow Farragut from American clipper ship *Great Admiral*; the scroll base is a replacement. H. without base 89 in. (225.4 cm.). Source: Sumner Pingree, Jr., Charles Weld Pingree, John R. Pingree, 58.1095.

29. David Glasgow Farragut (1801–1870) as Rear Admiral, a rank he held from 1862 to 1864. Lithograph after photograph by Mathew Brady. National Portrait Gallery, Smithsonian Institution, Washington, D.C.

In March 1866, less than a year after the launching of *Seminole,* a fire destroyed Campbell & Colby's rented shop and all of their tools, which, according to a newspaper account, "cannot be replaced except by importation."[26] They must have recovered the loss, for they were back making figureheads at least by 1869.

In 1873 Colby carved a portrait of himself for the schooner *John N. Colby,* built in Noank. The schooner *Abbie E. Campbell,* built in 1866 at the Maxson & Fish yard, was named for James Campbell's daughter. It appears, therefore, that these men and their trade were highly regarded in the area. In 1877 lack of work forced the firm to cease operation. Campbell moved to New York and then to San Francisco, but by 1888 was back in Mystic. Colby eventually moved to New London and continued his shipcarving business under the name of J. N. Colby & Co. However, the demand for this kind of work declined and by 1884 he was making cane umbrellas and "other such things of his own invention."[27]

Like the *Seminole,* the three-masted ship *Great Admiral* was classed as a medium clipper. It was built in 1869 by Robert E. Jackson in East Boston for William F. Weld, and was named in honor of the naval hero Admiral David Glasgow Farragut. Three years earlier, in 1866, Farragut had been the first man given the rank of full admiral by an Act of Congress. Weld's daughter, Anna Minot Weld, was to marry in 1870 George Hamilton Perkins, who had served under Farragut during the Civil War.[28]

This figurehead (Fig. 28) has long been attributed to John W. Anderson of New York (1834–1904).[29] It is not known if Farragut, who died the year after the launching, sat for the carving or if he ever saw the vessel. There were many pictures of the admiral, and judging from a print (Fig. 29) made from a photograph taken of him in 1864 in uniform, it is apparent that the carving is a good likeness.

30. Ship *Great Admiral*, launched in 1869 from Robert E. Jackson's East Boston shipyard, shown here in photograph by Thomas A. E. Luke, probably at Constitution Wharf, Boston, 1895-1900. Photograph: Peabody Museum of Salem, Massachusetts.

The *Great Admiral*, a favorite ship of her owners, was well maintained throughout her career and was referred to as "The Weld yacht."[30] A reminiscence of 1938 by H. H. Neligan who served aboard her in the 1890s includes a good account of the care taken with the figurehead:

> First chance after leaving port a pair of sheer legs was shipped on the lee side of the forecastle head, a tackle was hooked on to an eye-bolt between the Admiral's shoulders, some bolts were taken adrift, and the figure was hoisted on deck, to be stowed and bolted in his own locker under the forecastle head. It was the mate who took on himself to paint the admiral with a special enamel paint and real gold leaf. The mate also used to "gold leaf" the scroll work on her stem and counter, having a screen around him, while fixing the gold leaf; to keep the wind off.
>
> Her figure head and scroll work were works of art and greatly admired wherever she went and would always attract sightseers in Liverpool and Australia, even in the days when sailing ships were common to every port.[31]

A photograph of the figurehead on the bow (Fig. 30) shows the elaborate stem decoration with extensive areas obviously gold leafed. The figurehead itself appears to have a sheen, which may be due to the enamel paint used by the mate mentioned by Neligan.

In 1906 the *Great Admiral* was wrecked off the coast of Oregon. The figurehead was saved, but the scrollwork and shield were lost. For many years before coming to the Seaport in 1958 it stood in the Welds' garden in Maine. At the Seaport rot damage was repaired and a new scroll base was made.

31. Figurehead from British ship *Rhine* of 1886. H. 77 in. (195.6 cm.). Source: Mrs. Laurence J. Brengle, Sr., 51.4002.

Larger Merchant Ships

By the end of the 1860s, the heyday of the clipper ship was over. Bigger, stronger vessels were being built. The opening of the Suez Canal in 1869 ended the necessity for the long journey around the Cape of Good Hope. Larger cargoes required heavier ships with more capacity. The development of the steam engine for ocean-going vessels added reliability to schedules. Iron and steel hulls were stronger and more durable than wood. All of these innovations influenced ship design and ushered in the era of four- and five-masted ships and barks.

In the second half of the nineteenth century many large, multi-masted cargo vessels and screw steam passenger ships were launched from British shipyards. Figureheads graced the bows of many of these vessels, but they were becoming an anachronism. The figureheads, many of which may be seen in contemporary photographs, were neither portraits nor national symbols. They were usually life-size figures representing women in vaguely classical dress.

The Seaport has three figureheads from British-built merchant vessels. The figurehead from the three-masted iron ship *Rhine* is typical of this style. The *Rhine*, launched on 10 December 1886,[32] was one of seven vessels built by Russell & Co. in Greenock, Scotland, for James Nourse of London. The vessels of the Nourse fleet, built between 1884 and 1887, were all named for rivers and built for the coolie trade,[33] the transport of cheap unskilled laborers from Asia, especially India and China.

The figurehead represents a woman in classic dress holding a harp at her side with her left hand and with her right arm across her chest (Fig. 31). Some photographs of the ship show the figurehead apparently painted in a solid light color, while others show obvious contrasting shades, indicating that parts of the figurehead were painted in colors or gold leafed (Fig. 32). During restoration at the Seaport in 1951, at which time about three bushels of rotten wood were removed from the interior, traces of pale green paint were discovered beneath the aluminum color. The dress was repainted green with gold leaf on the trim and necklace.

An entry in the Russell cost book for the *Rhine* provides some documentation directly related to the figurehead (Fig. 33). On 30 November 1886, less than two weeks before launching, notes were made for payment for, among other services, the carving and gilding and "Reducing Head of Figure to clear Bowsprit."[34] Payment was made to John Roberts, but it is not known whether he was the actual carver or merely the one who fit the figurehead on the bow at the shipyard. The Greenock Directory of 1886 lists seven carvers, but Roberts' name is not among them.[35]

At the outbreak of World War I the *Rhine* was sold to U. S. interests and sailed out of Boston in the lumber trade with Argentina. After the war she carried jute from Calcutta. She was damaged by fire in 1920 and lay unused for several years until she was sold in 1923 at a United States marshal's sale to a Boston junk dealer, Marks Angel, for $975, and later was converted to a barge in New York.[36] Sometime between the marshal's sale and 1926 Laurence J. Brengle acquired the figurehead, which remained on the grounds of his residence in Maine until it was donated to the Seaport in 1951.

The *Rhine* figurehead bears many resemblances to an unidentified figurehead in the collection. This nearly full-length figure of a woman from the Tarkington estate is in the same pose with left arm at her side and right hand across her breast (Fig. 51). The flat wide collar, thick necklace, and gathered sleeves are all similar to those on the *Rhine* figurehead. The two figureheads are almost exactly the same size. These similarities indicate that the Tarkington figure may be of British origin and of the same period.

Another figurehead, the largest one in the collection, in the same style is from the three-masted steel-screw schooner *Magdalena* (Fig. 34) built in 1889 by R. Napier & Sons in Glasgow, for the Royal Mail Steam Packet Co. She is clad in a loose, belted robe, with her left hand raised to her chest — her right hand at her side holding a palm branch (Fig. 35). She is carved with no protruding limbs

32. Iron ship *Rhine*, built 1886 by Russell & Co., Greenock, Scotland; one of seven ships built for James Nourse and named for rivers. Photograph: National Maritime Museum, Greenwich, England.

33. The only reference to the figurehead in Russell & Co.'s cost book for *Rhine* notes payment to John Roberts for alterations shortly before launching. The figurehead was probably carved elsewhere and brought to the shipyard for fitting. Photograph: Glasgow University Archives, Lithgows, Ltd.

or accessories, and all ornament is flat and stylized. The absence of protrusions allowed the carving to withstand the rigors of life at sea with less chance of damage. The *Magdalena* was one of the last British liners to be built with a clipper bow. During World War I she was used for government service and was broken up some time after 1921.[37]

One case is known of a shipowner giving identity to his fleet not only by assigning similar names to the individual vessels but also by having a series of similar figureheads made. Between 1865 and 1892 Eyre, Evans Co. of Liverpool had seven vessels built in Scottish and English yards, and all were given East Indian names ending in "ore."[38] The four-masted bark *Balasore* built in 1892 at Barclay, Curle & Co. yard at Glasgow was one of these. Her figurehead is a nearly full-length figure of a bearded turbaned Indian holding a saber at his left side (Fig. 37). Photographs of the *Rajore* (Fig. 36) built in Southampton in 1882, the *Barcore* (Fig. 38) built at Stockton in 1884, and the *Indore* (Fig. 39) built in 1885 at Stockton all show figureheads that are remarkably similar. All of them have their left arms at their sides holding some sort of sword, and their right arms raised across their chests. It is safe to assume that the other three vessels also had turbaned figureheads.

34. Figurehead clearly visible on bow of screw steamer *Magdalena*, built 1889 by R. Napier & Sons, Glasgow, Scotland. Photograph: National Maritime Museum, Greenwich, England.

35. The largest figurehead in the collection is from the three-masted steel screw steamer *Magdalena*, built for the Royal Mail Steam Packet Co. H. 102 in. (258.4 cm.). Source: Harold H. Kynett, 54.1391.

36 (below). Figurehead on Eyre, Evans Co. ship *Rajore*, built ten years before *Balasore*. The turbaned figure is almost identical to the *Balasore* carving. Photograph: Mystic Seaport Museum, 50.982.

37. Figurehead from four-masted steel bark *Balasore*, built 1892 by Barclay, Curle & Co., Glasgow, Scotland, for Eyre, Evans Co. During her fifty-year career her name was changed to *Dalbek*, *Monongahela*, and back to *Balasore* when she was converted to a logging barge in the 1930s. H. 85 in. (215.2 cm.). Source: Powell River Co., Ltd., 49.2853.

38. (above). Iron ship *Barcore*, built 1884. The figurehead appears to resemble other Eyre, Evans Co. East Indian-style figureheads. Photograph: Peabody Museum of Salem, Massachusetts.

39. Another figurehead in the family of Eyre, Evans Co. "ore" vessels on the bow of the iron ship *Indore*, built 1885. Photograph: Mystic Seaport Museum, 50.1012.

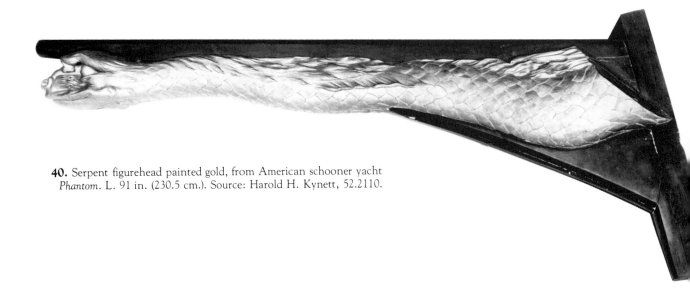

40. Serpent figurehead painted gold, from American schooner yacht
Phantom. L. 91 in. (230.5 cm.). Source: Harold H. Kynett, 52.2110.

Yachts

The lavish yachts of the late nineteenth and early twentieth centuries, built for
the industrialists and financiers of the era, were the luxury models of their
commercial counterparts. These vessels, sail as well as steam, wood and metal,
were designed inside and out to be fit for a king.

The earliest yacht figurehead in the collection, and perhaps the most
dramatic, is the scaly serpent from the schooner *Phantom* (Figs. 40, 41). *Phantom*
was built in 1865 in New York by J. B. Van Deusen for Henry George Stebbins
(1811–1881), who at one time was president of the New York Stock Exchange.
His yacht was the flagship of the New York Yacht Club from 1867 to 1870 and
in 1870 raced in the *America*'s Cup trial races, coming in seventh in corrected
time.[39] From photographs it appears that the figurehead's body was probably
nearly twice as long as that which survives today, with another several feet of
body extending back to serve as serpentine trailboards (Fig. 42).

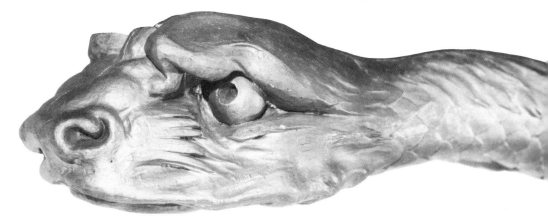

41. Detail of serpent figurehead from American schooner yacht *Phantom*.

50

42. Schooner yacht *Phantom* under sail, built 1865 by Joseph B. Van Deusen, New York, for H. G. Stebbins. The figurehead appears to be twice as long as what remains today, with a sinuous tail extending aft from the bow. Photograph: New York Yacht Club.

In 1879 the schooner was lengthened from 101 to 104 feet by Robert Palmer in Noank, Connecticut. In 1884 she was rebuilt by J. M. Bayles of Port Jefferson, New York, and in 1900 she was said to have become a houseboat and dropped out of the registers.[40]

In a more patriotic vein is the eagle from Jay Gould's steam yacht *Atalanta* (Fig. 43). This figurehead came to the Seaport with the trailboards with the yacht's name carved on them, a rare occurrence indeed. *Atalanta* was designed and built by William Cramp & Sons in Philadelphia in 1883. Considering that *Atalanta* was 228 feet long, her small eagle figurehead is modest by comparison.

43. Eagle figurehead and trailboards from three-masted iron screw schooner yacht *Atalanta*, designed and built by William Cramp & Sons, Philadelphia, 1883, for railroad tycoon Jay Gould. L. including trailboards 81 in. (205.1 cm.). Source: Marian C. Coffin, in memory of her mother, Mrs. Julian Coffin, 49.753.

51

44. Steel screw schooner yacht *Iolanda*, designed by Cox & King, built by Ramage and Ferguson, Leith, Scotland, 1908, for American philanthropist and yachtsman Morton F. Plant. The seven-foot figurehead is dwarfed by the long trailboards. Photograph: The Mariners' Museum, Newport News, Virginia.

The 318-foot steam yacht *Iolanda* was built in 1908 by Ramage & Ferguson in Leith, Scotland, for the philanthropist Morton Freeman Plant (1852–1918) who had an estate in Groton, Connecticut. *Iolanda* at the time of her launching was one of the largest private yachts in the world, and was frequently seen on the Thames River off New London and on Long Island Sound (Fig. 44).

The figurehead in the Seaport's collection (Fig. 45) is probably the second one carved for the yacht, a nearly exact copy of the original. The original figurehead at one time belonged to a Seattle restaurant and was mounted over the doorway (Fig. 46). It now belongs to the Museum of History and Industry in Seattle. Both are full-length women in flowing robes with arms held close to their bodies in the same style as the figureheads from *Rhine* and *Magdalena*.

This figurehead was known as "Lost Lady" when it was acquired by the Museum. It was later identified by Robert D. Huntington, Jr., who recognized it as coming from the yacht of his grandmother, Mrs. Moses Taylor of Rhode Island. Morton Plant had sold *Iolanda* in 1911, and there followed a series of owners. By 1931 she was owned by Mrs. Taylor, who had the original figurehead removed because of dry rot. At that time Mrs. Taylor commissioned a copy to be made, and according to her grandson it was carved by a Mr. Meadows of Shirley, England. Nothing is known of Mr. Meadows, but comparison of his copy to photographs of the original makes it apparent that he made a faithful copy, varying only slightly the neck ornaments and altering the facial features.

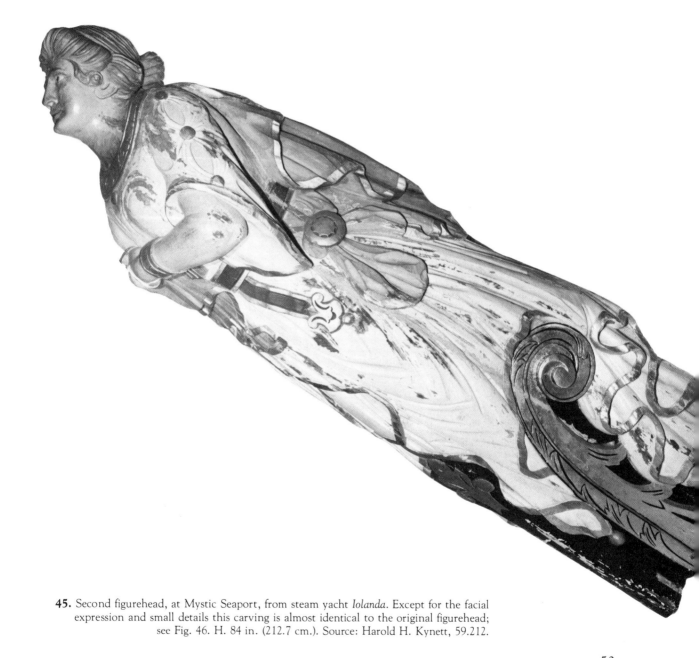

45. Second figurehead, at Mystic Seaport, from steam yacht *Iolanda*. Except for the facial expression and small details this carving is almost identical to the original figurehead; see Fig. 46. H. 84 in. (212.7 cm.). Source: Harold H. Kynett, 59.212.

During World War II *Iolanda* was converted for war use by the British Navy and renamed H.M.S. *White Bear*. In 1940, according to Mr. Huntington, all her fittings were moved and stored at Camper & Nicholsons in Southampton. The figurehead was acquired by a London dealer shortly after the war, and the Seaport acquired it in 1959 from a gallery in London.

46. Figurehead believed to be the original one from steam yacht *Iolanda*, photographed in the 1950s when it was mounted outside a Seattle restaurant. Museum of History and Industry, Seattle, Washington.

Unlike the previous three yachts, the iron ship *Joseph Conrad* began her career as a Danish training ship. Built in 1882 by Burmeister & Wain in Copenhagen and originally named the *Georg Stage*, she carried a wooden bust figurehead of her namesake. Later the wood carving was replaced by a metal one.[41] After fifty-two years of service in Denmark as the *Georg Stage* she was bought by Alan Villiers in 1934 and renamed *Joseph Conrad*. Villiers commissioned the noted type and book designer Bruce Rogers (1870–1957) to carve a head of Conrad for the bow in 1935. When Huntington Hartford owned the *Joseph Conrad* from 1936 to 1939 he used it as a private yacht. Hartford had Bruce Rogers' figurehead replaced with a bronze copy, the fourth to adorn the ship, and it is this copy (Fig. 47) which was on the ship when it arrived at Mystic Seaport and which is on her now.

In 1947 part of the trailboards were lost at sea and replacements were carved by Clark Voorhees of Old Lyme, Connecticut, some time between 1949 and 1951. It is not known if those lost at sea were original to the *Georg Stage*, but photographs of the ship show them to be similar if not identical.

47. Figurehead now on the steel ship *Joseph Conrad*, a bronze copy of the wood Conrad head by Bruce Rogers. H. 23 1/2 in. (59.7 cm.). Source: United States Maritime Commission, 47.1948 (vessel).

Chapter 4

The Collection: Unidentified Figureheads

Most of the Seaport's figureheads are from unidentified vessels, but they nevertheless merit study. They are of many styles, from small portrait busts to large full-length symbolic figures. Examination reveals how the carvers attached arms and how they shaped the figure to fit the bow. Comparisons with similar figureheads in our own and other collections help to date them and to determine probable countries of origin.

Bust of a Woman

The absence of a lacing piece and visible bolt holes has cast doubt on the authenticity of this figurehead (Fig. 48). However, it is apparent that there once was a space between the two side scrolls that was later filled in with a new piece of wood. This alteration probably covered the bolt hole on the back. On the front the hole has probably been covered by later repainting or is hidden under the brooch.

    The obvious signs of alteration and the bust's unmistakable resemblance to the *Eunice H. Adams* figurehead discussed in the previous chapter (Fig. 49), indicate that this unidentified woman is undoubtedly a figurehead. The collars, brooches, and shoulder drapery are alike on both carvings. The hair of the unidentified bust is carved in the same linear fashion, and a rosette similar to ones on the billet scrolls of both figures is at the center of the bun. Unlike the

48 (opposite). Figurehead bust of a woman, probably American, mid-19th century. H. 16 in. (40.6 cm.) Source: Laurence J. Brengle, Jr., William C. Brengle, Mrs. Thomas S. Gates, Jr., 53.87.

49. Figurehead from American schooner, later brig, *Eunice H. Adams*, of 1845. H. 17 3/4 in. (45.1 cm.). Source: Charles Francis Adams, Jr., Mrs. Henry S. Morgan, 56.745.

carving of the Adams bust, there is a suggestion of a comb on the left side of the head. The alteration mentioned above, fitting a piece of wood between the side scrolls, was probably made after the figurehead was removed from the vessel so that it could be set on a shelf or pedestal.

These two carvings share features in common with the following figure-head in the collection.

Bust of a Man

The donor's records called this figurehead "Mr. Roache" (Fig. 50), and at one time it was thought to have come from a whaler named *William Rotch*, but subsequent research has not revealed a vessel by that name with a figurehead.

The bust and lacing piece are carved from one piece of wood. The wood has split vertically from the back toward the center core, and the left shoulder

50. Figurehead bust of a man, probably American, mid-19th century. With shoulder drapery and billet rosettes, it is similar to the bust of a woman and *Eunice H. Adams* figureheads; see Figs. 48, 49. H. 19 3/4 in. (50.1 cm.). Source: Weston Howland, 47.1177.

has been re-attached. A bolt hole through the center of the lacing piece and the body emerges on the shirt front and is disguised by a decorative pin. A new piece of wood has been bolted to the underside of the base of the man, but traces of a notch for fitting over the stem are evident. Repainting of the bust before its arrival at the Seaport in 1947 has altered the man's facial features, leaving him without the delicacy of expression of the two women.

This bust, the *Eunice H. Adams* figurehead, and the unidentified bust of a woman all share similar shoulder drapery and circular side billet scrolls with center rosettes. The man's hair style is fuller than that of the two women, but it is carved with the same narrow linear grooves.

Because of their similarities to the known figurehead from the *Adams* the two unidentified busts may be attributed to an American carver around 1845. The two unidentified busts are probably good likenesses of individuals, and it is very likely that they are from small vessels that bore their names.

Full-Length Woman

In pose and dress this full-length carving of a woman (Fig. 51) resembles closely the *Rhine* figurehead discussed in the previous chapter (Fig. 31). It seems reasonable to consider this unknown woman to be from a British vessel of the 1880s.

The donor, recalling when the carving was owned by the writer Booth Tarkington, wrote that the figurehead was "found lying on her side in a chicken yard near Portland, Maine. Then painted white with black eyes and lips, her present patina dates from 1930."[1] Since then she has been repainted, and her original colors are unknown.

The lacing piece, carved with the figure from one piece of wood, extends forty-six inches from the middle of the back to the base and is indented in the figure's back so that the carving could fit snugly around the abutting timber on the ship. A large bolt hole goes through the figure, and a bung is visible on the front a foot below the buckle. Farther below, there is a smaller metal fastening still lodged in the figure.

In place of carved billet scrolls on both sides below the lower hem are flat areas painted black with gold-painted curving leaf designs. The leaves are slightly grooved to indicate veins.

Like the *Rhine* carving, this figure's pose is contained, with arms held close to the body. On the front the lower dress folds begin to form the shape of the ship's stem piece.

Fragment of a Woman

Unrestored, this figurehead fragment is one of the most beautiful and interesting carvings in the collection. Only the top thirty-five inches of this larger-than-life-size figure remain today (Fig. 52). The lower part, probably badly worn and damaged, was sawed off at some time in the past.

In 1969 the carving was treated by a wax immersion process to halt the growth of dry rot and to solidify and preserve intact what remained of the carving. During the six-hour immersion the wooden figure absorbed over fourteen pounds of wax, mostly in the lower deteriorated areas.

No attempt has been made to repaint the figure, and much of the surface is bare wood revealing fine carving detail (Fig. 53). The shoulder straps and front bodice are carved in relief. Broad circular motifs and smaller bands of geometric patterns are boldly incised to indicate the dress fabric. Two strands of beads and two pairs of arm bracelets are also carved. It is obvious that the carver knew the figure would be seen from a distance. The scale of the head, shoulders, and chest is heroic. The facial expression is firm yet natural and gentle, and the fragment of the right hand is skillfully carved and lifelike in proportion.

The lacing piece was carved with the figure from the same piece of wood. Originally it probably protruded from the back but has since been chiseled down flush with the back of the figure. There is evidence of part of a bolt hole

51. Three-quarter-length figurehead, stylistically like the one from *Rhine* (see Fig. 31); probably European, last quarter of the 19th century. H. 77 in. (195.6 cm.). Source: Estate of Booth Tarkington, 51.3358.

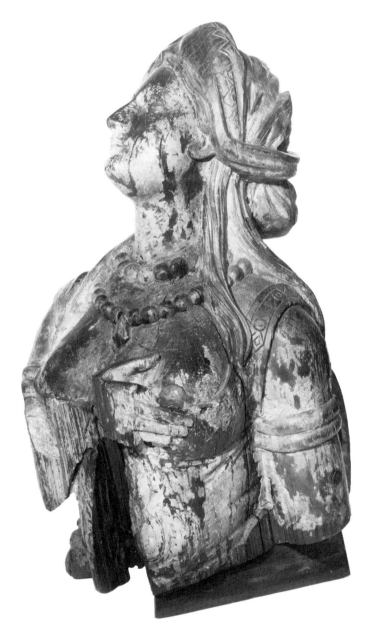

52. Fragment of figurehead, originally probably full-length. H. 35 in. (88.9 cm.). Source: Estate of Booth Tarkington, 51.3357.

53 (opposite). Detail of Fig. 52. Skillful carving is apparent on the unrestored surfaces of this figurehead.

and iron rust on the front at the lower edge of the carving. Traces of paint, some nearly 1/8 inch thick, reveal many layers and several colors. Much gold leaf or gold paint still adheres to areas of the dress and turban.

Judging from the vaguely classical attire, this figure probably represented a symbolic character rather than an individual. With her upturned head, right arm across her breast, and her dress she resembles the large figureheads like *Rhine*, *Magdalena* (Fig. 35), and *Iolanda* (Fig. 45).

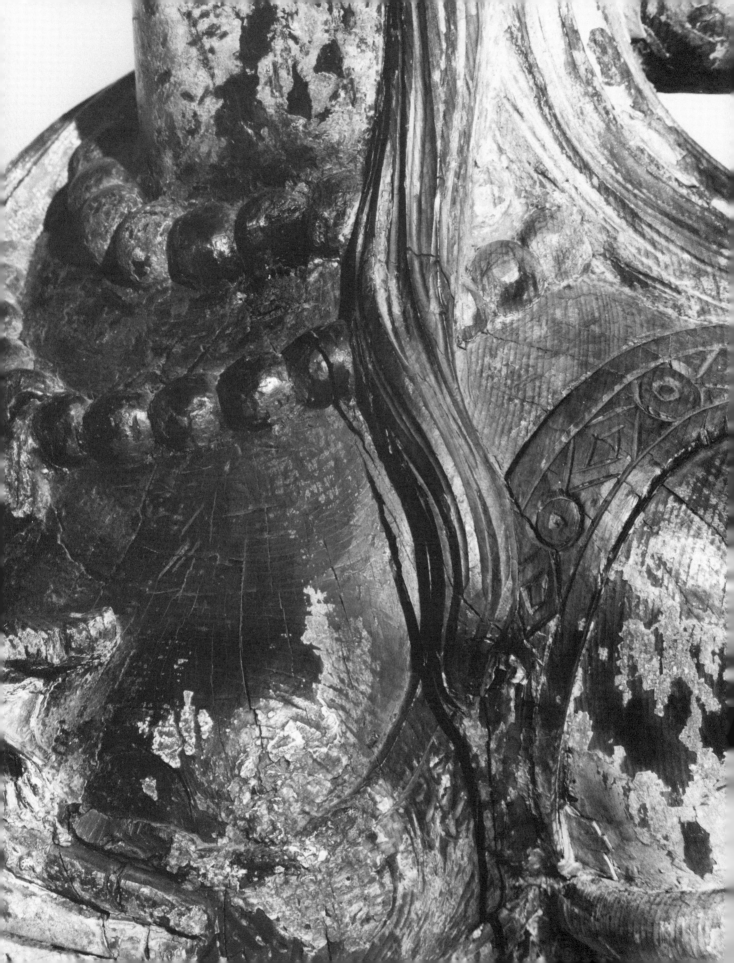

54, 55. Figurehead, Woman with Binoculars. H. 37 in. (94 cm.). Source:
Mrs. Harriet Greenman Stillman, 33.85.

58 (below).
Figurehead known as
"Lizzie" in pose and
costume closely
resembles Woman
with Binoculars.
H. 48 in. (121.9 cm.).
The Mariners'
Museum, Newport
News, Virginia.

56. Detail of hat, Woman with Binoculars.

57. Detail of hat, "Lizzie." This figurehead and the Woman with Binoculars may be by the same carver.

Woman with Binoculars

The Woman with Binoculars was given by Harriet Greenman Stillman, who purchased it for the Museum from a Boston antique dealer in 1933 (Figs. 54, 55). At that time it was called "Lady Blessington" and was thought to be from a ship by that name built in Belfast, Maine, in 1855, an attribution that cannot now be verified.

There has been some deterioration of the wood, especially along the bottom, and it is obvious that an attempt was made at repairing the left hand and the purse it holds. The figure had been repainted at some time before its acquisition. The figure and the lacing piece are carved from one piece of wood. Two circular cuts, one above the other, on the center front of the skirt show where bungs covered the bolt holes. The lower hole is visible on the lacing piece on back, but the upper hole has been obscured by attempts to cover it. Several inches have probably been sawed off the bottom, since there are no traces of the mortise that would have been cut to fit over a corresponding tenon on the top of the stem piece of the vessel.

This figurehead may be compared to another unidentified one known as "Lizzie," in the Mariners' Museum (Fig. 58). Both three-quarter-length figures are in the same pose, holding an object in each hand with the right hand across the chest. Their clothing is similar, from the pointed, turned-up sleeve cuffs to the hats, each of which has a bow in front and a feather on the right side lying on the brim (Figs. 56, 57). The Seaport's figure has a cord hatband, whereas

"Lizzie" has a cord holding her hair back in a loose bun. The billetheads at the bases of both carvings are simple scrolls with traces of leaf decorations at the outer edges. "Lizzie" is eleven inches taller than the Woman with Binoculars. The remarkable similarities between these two figureheads indicate that they may have been made by the same carver or at least may be from the same region. "Lizzie," acquired by the Mariners' Museum in 1935, was said to have come from a collection of twelve British figureheads.

Woman with a Comb

At the time it was acquired by the Museum this half-length figurehead (Fig. 59) was said to have come from Danvers, Massachusetts. Although we have no further information concerning its origin, the carving may be compared to another unidentified figurehead in a private collection (Fig. 60). The pose, dress,

59. Figurehead, Woman with a Comb. The deeply carved features could be easily seen from a distance. H. 44 in. (111.8 cm.). Source: Harold H. Kynett, 48.20.

60. Figurehead similar to Woman with a Comb, with hip drapery, buckled belt, pointed collar, gathered sleeves, and ornate hair arrangement. Present location unknown. Pl. 28 from Hornung, *Treasury of American Design* (New York [1972]), p. 19.

hair styles of the 1820s, and base drapery are remarkably similar. The base of the Seaport's figure was sawed off at one time and originally probably resembled the base of the other carving. On the Seaport's figure the base notch, which almost certainly was present on the full carving, is now gone, and the lower arcs of the side scrolls and front base leaves, the tops of which are visible below the drapery, have been sawed off. The underside shows signs of rot, which suggests that the lower part of the base had badly deteriorated.

The figure, including the lacing piece, is carved from one piece of wood. The lacing piece, rather than protruding from the figure, is slightly recessed in the figure's back, and dress folds extend back hiding the lacing piece from the side view. There is one bolt hole in the middle of the lacing piece; on the front the hole is on the belt, and it was probably covered by a buckle that is now missing. The top of the comb, a separate piece, is probably a replacement, but the teeth are carved on the figure's head.

61. Figurehead, half-length man with missing arm, ca. 1830s. The raised right shoulder and stretch creases on the jacket indicate that the detachable right arm was probably raised. H. 36 1/2 in. (92.7 cm.). Source: Harold H. Kynett, 52.1205.

Half-Length Man with Detached Arm

When this figure (Fig. 61) was acquired by the Museum it was believed to represent Alexander Hamilton, but the clothes are in the style of the 1830s, more than a quarter century after Hamilton's death. However, the carefully carved facial features suggest that it is a portrait.

The right shoulder has a groove on which the missing arm would have been attached. Protruding limbs would not last long at sea, and therefore they were often removed and stowed below decks after leaving port. The unnatural slope of the left shoulder and awkward attachment of the arm suggest that the left arm is a later replacement.

The torso and the lacing piece are carved from one piece of wood. The small front billet scroll is a separate piece. A bolt hole through the lacing piece and body emerges between the two right-hand buttons. The five-inch-high notch between the billet scrolls fit over the stem piece, giving the figure lateral stability.

Gray Man

The clothing and hair of the figurehead shown in Fig. 61 are similar in style to those of a figurehead known as the Gray Man (Fig. 62), indicating that it too is probably from the 1830s. This carving is covered with a thin coat of bluish-gray paint over the entire surface, under which are traces of white paint.

At some time the base of this figurehead was altered, probably to make the carving look more like a marble portrait bust. As on the small bust of a woman (Fig. 48) the center notch has been filled with wooden plugs. Probably several inches of the base of the Gray Man have been removed. There are no through bolt holes visible on the figure, and it is probable that they were on the cut-off part of the base. Since the figure is small and lightweight, attachment to the stem would have been easy.

62. Bust figurehead, Gray Man, ca. 1830s. The hair style and clothes are of the same era as those of the figurehead in Fig. 61; delicate carving is visible beneath the thin layer of bluish gray paint. H. 22 in. (55.9 cm.). Source: Harold H. Kynett, 52.1206.

63. Figurehead, three-quarter-length woman. H. 27 in. (68.6 cm.). Source: Harold H. Kynett, 50.2874.

Three-Quarter-Length Woman

The vessel from which this small, compact three-quarter-length figurehead of a woman came is unknown (Fig. 63). The figure and lacing piece are carved together from one piece of wood. To solve the problem of protruding limbs the artist carved the figure so that the arms become part of the design of the skirt folds where they are gathered at the waist. In spite of minor restorations and crude repainting the figurehead retains some of its former charm.

On the bottom there is the original cut-out for fitting the figurehead over a bow timber. There are two holes in the back of the lacing piece. The smaller one at the top was probably added at a later date after the figurehead was separated from the ship. The larger one below still has a metal rod through it, which undoubtedly is the original one that secured the carving to the ship. The other end of the rod comes out at the waist, and the hole is covered by a dress ornament.

The metal rod shows up clearly in X-ray photographs (Fig. 64). Numerous twentieth-century finishing nails are also visible, especially at bust level and around the billet scrolls. These nails are later additions, probably attempts at restoration. No metal fastening is visible in the area of the upper hole in the lacing piece.

64. X-ray photographs of the figurehead shown in Fig. 63. Nails, presumably used for repairs, are in the hair, bust, and scroll; the horizontal shadow shows the presence of the metal drift used to attach the figurehead to the vessel. Photograph: Clifford Crane, conservator, Fogg Art Museum, Cambridge, Massachusetts, 1981.

65. Figurehead, Woman with Roses, called "Belva Lockwood" by her previous owner. H. 59 1/2 in. (151.1 cm.). Source: Harold H. Kynett, 51.651.

66. Portrait of Belva Ann Lockwood (1830–1917) from 1884 campaign card. Her features and expression are remarkably like those of the figurehead shown in Fig. 65. Division of Political History, National Museum of American History, Smithsonian Institution, Washington, D.C.

Woman with Roses

This full-length figurehead of a woman holding a bouquet of roses came to the Museum in 1951 with the name "Belva Lockwood" (Fig. 65). No conclusive evidence has been found to link the figurehead with a vessel of that name, but it is interesting to speculate on the possibility.

Belva Ann Bennett Lockwood (1830–1917) was a lawyer and a leader in the women's suffrage movement in the United States. She was twice a candidate for President, nominated in 1884 and 1888 by the Equal Rights Party.[2] Photographs of her in middle age (Fig. 66) dressed in the style of the 1880s look remarkably like the Woman with Roses. Although the figurehead has not been positively identified, there is little doubt that it is a portrait. The determined expression and purposeful stride indicate that the carver made a likeness of a specific individual.

At first glance the figure seems to have been carved in the round, because the lacing piece has been removed. Inspection, however, reveals the outline of the original lacing piece, and there are five metal bolts visible within the outline. It extends from the shoulders to the base and varies in width from 5-1/2 to 7-1/2 inches. The lower part of the base has been sawed off, eliminating the slot under the billethead.

In profile, the straight line from the hips to the base on back indicates that this part of the carving was flush against the ship. The front of the figure from the knee to the base is straight also, but it is apparent that the extended left foot and forward part of the billethead are missing. Beside repainting, there have been minor restorations to the nose, left hand, and possibly to the flowers. The figure is solid except for a space between the body and left arm.

73

67. Figurehead, Woman with Beads. H. 74 in. (187.9 cm.). Source: Mr. and Mrs. Stanley Livingston, Jr., 58.1290.

The Woman with Beads

The Woman with Beads (Fig. 67) is clad in vaguely sixteenth-century dress and has two long braids reaching to the backs of her knees. The shape of the lower part of the figurehead, with exposed billet scrolls on the sides and shallow, wide dress folds tapering down to the stem piece on front, is similar to other large three-quarter to full-length figureheads representing classical or exotic figures. Among them are the figureheads from *Rhine* (Fig. 31) of 1886 and *Balasore* (Fig. 37) of 1892. It is possible, judging from the similarities of style and shape, that the Woman with Beads, like these two, also dates from the end of the nineteenth century and is of British origin.

Characteristic of this figurehead type from the last decades of the Victorian era is the theatrical attire and rigidity of pose. The Woman with Beads probably represents a romanticized historic or literary figure, very different from the individualized Eunice Adams and Admiral Farragut figureheads that represent real people.

Two one-inch diameter threaded bolts protrude from the lacing piece on back, one at hip level and one at knee level, and the entire lacing piece reaches to the shoulder blades. Repairs to the carving have obliterated evidence of the bolts on front. Only the upper half of the billet scroll remains, and part of the ribbon at the end of the left braid has been sawed off, presumably when the figurehead was removed from the vessel. Restoration attempts have distorted details of the figure's face, neck, and bust.

"St. George"

A previous owner of this figurehead (Fig. 68) called it "St. George" and believed it to be from a British merchant ship of the same name. As is the case with most of the figureheads that remain today, the name survives in quotation marks until positive ship identification is found. The clothes and accessories of this figurehead, however, strongly suggest that the carving represents St. George, the patron saint of England, the Red Cross Knight. In the absence of conclusive evidence the figurehead is tentatively attributed to Britain's last sail training ship, *St. George*. Photographs of the vessel at a distance (too dim to reproduce) show its figurehead in profile, and it is tantalizingly similar to the carving in the Museum.

The *St. George* was built in 1890 as a yacht for the English yachtsman Ernest James Wythes by Ramage & Ferguson, Ltd., Leith, Scotland. The auxiliary three-masted topsail schooner was 191 feet long. She is said to have been well built, with teak sheathing over iron frames. During World War I she was in service for the British government in the Mediterranean Sea. In 1919 Devitt & Moore purchased her and refitted her for use as a training ship in conjunction with the Nautical College at Pangbourne, England. Several years later she was sold to the Scientific Research Expedition, and in 1924 sailed to the South Seas with an expedition collecting animal and plant specimens. In 1928 she was broken up and sold for scrap.[3]

The massive figurehead was secured to its vessel by at least four through fastenings that are still visible on the front of the figure. The lacing piece on the back has been covered with a piece of metal sheathing. The metal shield attached to the left arm with four metal fastenings covers a red cross painted on the figure's chest. The carving of the chain mail is detailed and lifelike. The billet scrolls, probably originally gilded, have the usual incised leaf designs and are now painted white.

68 (opposite). Figurehead known as "St. George," possibly from a British three-masted topsail schooner of that name, built as a yacht and later used for sail training. H. 84 in. (212.7 cm.). Source: Harold H. Kynett, 56.686.

69. Figurehead believed to be from the Cunard Line passenger steamer *Aleppo*, built 1865, Glasgow, Scotland. H. 84 in. (212.7 cm.). Source: Harold H. Kynett, 46.230.

"Aleppo"

This figurehead came to the Seaport identified as "Aleppo" and was thought to be from a British vessel of that name (Fig. 69). The name persists in the absence of concrete evidence. Although the carving has not been positively identified with any of the British *Aleppos* of the nineteenth century, the exotic figure is similar in style to the turbaned *Balasore* (Fig. 37) and may be from a vessel of the second half of the nineteenth century. Both figureheads wear turbans and wide sashes, and both carry objects in their left hands. Also both have lower drapery with folds masking the transition from the figurehead to the vessel.

The figurehead has obviously undergone a number of attempted restorations. As was the case with the Woman with Roses, the upper part of the lacing piece on "Aleppo" has been cut off completely, and the figure now appears to be carved in the round. Only the lower portion of the lacing piece below the knees remains. A five-by-four-inch square plug is clearly visible on the front above the lower drapery, and this plug undoubtedly hides one of the metal through fastenings necessary for attaching the figurehead to the vessel. In addition to the lacing piece alterations, there have been some repairs to the arms and hands. The fastening just below the neck on front is modern.

There are two bungs, one on each side of the figure at knee height, level with the square plug. It is possible that these cover a lateral fastening that was used for support. It may be noted that another figurehead in the collection, "Abigail," also has a lateral through hole (Fig. 70).

Of the several vessels named *Aleppo*, one is a possible candidate. The 292-foot passenger steamer built for the Cunard Line in 1865 by J. & G. Thompson, Glasgow, Scotland, and scrapped in 1909 was one of several sister-ships in the Liverpool-Mediterranean service. A photograph exists showing a white full-length figurehead in place, but it is too dim to determine whether or not there are enough similarities to the surviving carving.

70 (opposite). Figurehead known as "Abigail." H. 78 1/2 in. (199.4 cm.). Source: Mrs. Albert H. Ely, Oliver B. Jennings, Mrs. Henry C. Taylor, 48.1133.

71. Figurehead possibly from British second rate ship of 1824, H.M.S. *Asia*. H. 55 1/2 in. (141 cm.). Source: Mrs. Harriet Greenman Stillman, 33.41.

"Asia"

The British were building ships in India at least by the mid-seventeenth century, and the decorative carving for the vessels may have been done in India by native artisans. Materials and labor were inexpensive and of good quality.[4] India played an enormous role in the economic and social history of the British Empire, and, not surprisingly, this influence is apparent even in figureheads. The *Balasore* figurehead (Fig. 37) and the "Aleppo" carving are examples of this. A third figurehead in this Oriental group is "Asia" (Fig. 71).

This figurehead was the first one acquired by the Museum. Said by a previous owner to have come from a vessel named *Asia*, the figure may be either a portrait of an individual or an idealized representation of an Asian. It may be from the second rate ship of eighty-four guns, H.M.S. *Asia*, launched in Bombay, India, in January 1824 (Fig. 72). An Admiralty catalog of pictures and artifacts published in 1911 lists a figurehead from this vessel, a bust figure of a rajah, six feet high.[5] The Seaport's figurehead is only 4-1/2 feet high, but it is possible that part of the base has been removed. Photographs and paintings of the ship, although varied and indistinct, show an upright turbaned bust at the stem.

72. H.M.S. *Asia*, launched at Bombay, India, 1824. The dark-skinned half-length figurehead that looks like the figurehead "Asia" is on the bow. Photograph: National Maritime Museum, Greenwich, England.

73. Of the same era as H.M.S. *Asia* with a similar figurehead is the British training ship *Foudroyant*, built as the H.M.S. *Trincomalee* in Bombay, 1817, and now located at Portsmouth, England. Reproduced from a postcard, with permission from the Foudroyant Trust. Source: Richard Orr, 55.1090.7.

The figurehead is now weak and fragile. The last restoration work done on it was in the 1930s just prior to its acquisition by the Museum. That the figure once had arms or shoulder decorations is apparent by the shoulder notches. The body of the figure is almost perfectly symmetrical, and we can guess that the arms when attached probably looked somewhat like those on H.M.S. *Foudroyant* (ex-*Trincomalee*) built in Bombay in 1817 (Fig. 73). Hatch lines on "Asia" where the arms would have been attached at the shoulder indicate more decoration, possibly a lion's mane or a rope design (Fig. 74). The style of figurehead is relatively common, and many similar examples are known in other museums.

The lower front part of the figurehead below the belt has been smoothed down and the decoration obliterated. There is an outline of a notch, 9-1/4 by 3-1/2 inches, which is now filled in, at the center of the lower front. The original billet scrolls no longer exist. The carving on the back is not as detailed as it is on the front, except for the turban, the head, and the top of the garment. The lacing piece has been shaved down and repainted. On the back are two holes, one of which has been filled in, which correspond to two bungs on the front, above and below the belt.

74. Detail of "Asia" showing notch and carving at the shoulder, where the arm with sleeve decoration was attached.

75. Figurehead of helmeted warrior believed to be from the British frigate H.M.S. *Orlando* of 1858. White pine. H. 68 in. (172.7 cm.). Source: Mrs. Harriet Greenman Stillman, 34.83.

76 (opposite). British frigate H.M.S. *Orlando*, built at Pembroke Dock, 1858. The figurehead on the bow may be the one in the Seaport's collection. Photograph: National Maritime Museum, Greenwich, England.

"Orlando"

Another unidentified figurehead in the collection, known as "Orlando," also fits into the category of Oriental or exotic figureheads. Known by its name because of the two-inch wedge-carved letters on the left face of the lacing piece, H. M. S. ORLANDO, this figurehead (Fig. 75) is similar to "Asia" in pose. The armored warrior wearing a plumed helmet was a popular theme for eighteenth- and nineteenth-century British warship figureheads, and the many surviving ones include *Canopus* of 1787, *Ajax* of 1809, and *Bellerophon* II of 1818.[6] Several Royal Navy vessels in the nineteenth century were named *Orlando*. Identification through pictures has thus far been inconclusive, but a photograph of the 300-foot wood screw frigate H.M.S. *Orlando* built at Pembroke dock in 1858 shows a white bust-length figurehead that resembles the Museum's carving (Fig. 76).

The lacing piece, which appears to be part of the same piece of white pine from which the figure is carved, is still in place.[7] The bottom edge of the drapery in front projects slightly from the billet scroll, and there is a notch that might have been for some part of the standing rigging. The leafy gilded billetheads are boldly carved in high relief.

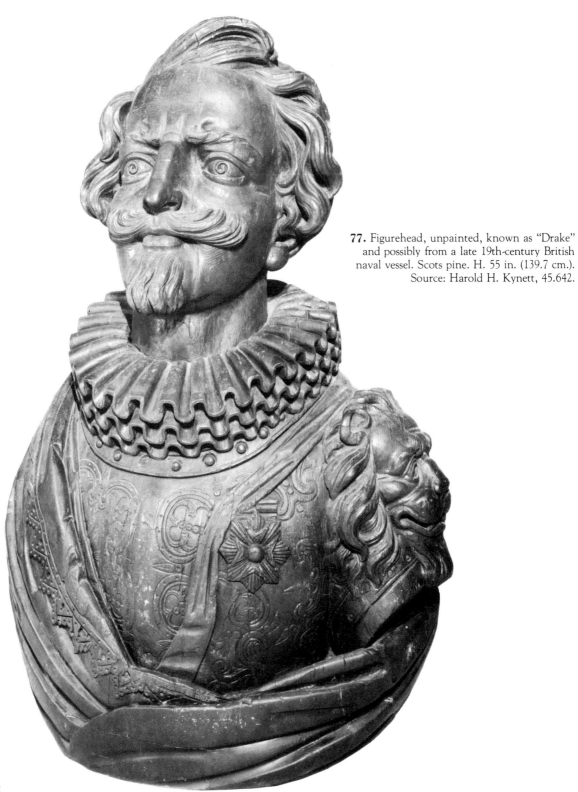

77. Figurehead, unpainted, known as "Drake" and possibly from a late 19th-century British naval vessel. Scots pine. H. 55 in. (139.7 cm.). Source: Harold H. Kynett, 45.642.

78. Bust figurehead on bow of British steam frigate H.M.S. *Raleigh*, built 1873, is similar in style to "Drake." Photograph: National Maritime Museum, Greenwich, England.

"Drake"

The magnificent carving known as "Drake" (Fig. 77) is unique in the Seaport's collection of figureheads for two reasons. The 4-1/2-foot-high figure is the largest bust carving in the collection, its height exceeding the dimensions of some of the full-length figureheads, and the carving is the only one in the Museum that shows no signs of ever having been painted. It has a dark patina of age, possibly due to an oil finish. Carved of Scots pine, the figurehead is undoubtedly of British origin, but no further identification has as yet been made.[8]

The figurehead was at one time in the collection of Charles T. Jeffery of Philadelphia, who allegedly purchased it in England. It was a featured item in an undated Samuel T. Freeman & Co. (Philadelphia) auction catalog. Listed as "Drake," it was not attributed to a specific vessel.

The carving bears some similarities to the figurehead from the British steam frigate of 1873 H.M.S. *Raleigh* (Fig. 78). This is also a large bust figure, and it was mounted on the straight stem of the vessel. It is probable that "Drake" was mounted in an upright position on a similar vessel of that period.

The figure represents a man in Elizabethan-style dress and looks not unlike some portraits of the eminent navigator of the period, Sir Francis Drake. It could, however, be the later Sir Walter Raleigh or some other prominent person of that period. There have been numerous British naval and merchant vessels of both names.

The carving is deftly executed. The hair, ruffled collar, facial features, and lion on the left shoulder are cut in deep relief (Fig. 79), while the surface details of the vest are incised in precise low relief. Pieces of wood have been added to fill out the figure, most notably the back of the head, which is secured with two large bolts. The carving is not as detailed on the back of the body, indicating that the figure was intended to be seen only from the front. A lacing notch is cut into the back of the figure, and there is a square hole in the bottom measuring 7 by 11 by 13-1/2 inches. There are several green patinaed metal bolts and some empty bolt holes visible in the bottom notch.

79. Collar and shoulder on "Drake"; clothing details are not carved on the back of the figurehead.

80. Sisters, double figurehead from an unidentified vessel. H. without base 37 in. (94 cm.). Source: Mary B. Behrend, 57.358.

Sisters

Another unusual figurehead in the collection is the one of two little girls, known as the Sisters. Very few double figureheads exist today, despite the number of nineteenth-century vessels with double names, such as *Mary & Elizabeth*, *Thomas & Henry*, not to mention *Two Sisters* and *Three Brothers*. The Sisters (Fig. 80) was purchased by the donor in Salem, Massachusetts, but whether it is from an American or foreign vessel is not known.

At least three other double figureheads are known, two of which are in European museums. One, thought to be from a French vessel named *Pauline et Marie* wrecked in 1867, was recently rediscovered and is now in the Sjöfartsmuseet in Göteborg, Sweden.[9] It is only half a foot taller and resembles the Sisters in pose (Fig. 81). The girls in both carvings are joined at their sides and are poised as if to begin dancing. The other two known double figureheads are of man and woman couples. One is at the Altonaer Museum in Hamburg, Germany.

81. Double figurehead said to be from the French schooner *Pauline et Marie*, wrecked 1867 on the northwest coast of Denmark. H. 44 1/2 in. (113 cm.). Sjöfartsmuseet i Göteborg, Sweden.

82 (opposite). Danish carver Henrik Julius Møen with his double figurehead. The pose, dress, lace details, and curled hair closely resemble those on the Sisters. Probably photographed in the 1850s. Photograph: Handels- og Søfartsmuseet pa Kronborg, Denmark.

83. Detail of distinctive lace trim and tight curls on the Sisters.

The other, by the Danish carver Henrik Julius Møen (1802–1881), is lost, and our only knowledge of it is through a photograph taken in the 1850s (Fig. 82). There are similarities between the triangular lace trim on the Sisters' skirts and pantaloons and that on Møen's double figurehead. Two other Møen carvings, a bust of a woman and a full-length girl, both have the same lace details. The Sisters' tightly curled locks of hair (Fig. 83) have been compared in style to the hair treatment in other Møen carvings.[10] These resemblances are intriguing but at this point are inconclusive.

Several conclusions may be made from physical examination of the carving. In the past the figurehead was called the twins, but it is obvious that although the girls do look alike, one is taller than the other and their faces are different. Repainting has obscured their differences. The two figures are carved

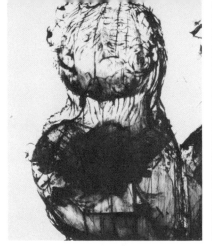

84. X-ray photographs of the Sisters, showing the presence of metal rods through the skirts connecting the bodies. Photograph: Clifford Crane, conservator, Fogg Art Museum, Cambridge, Massachusetts, 1981.

separately and in the round except at their joining and the lacing slot. They are pinned together side to side through their skirts with two iron rods, which are visible in X-ray photographs (Fig. 84). Four bungs, two on each skirt front, show where the rods are covered.

The base and feet are replacements, as are the awkwardly clasped hands. Photographs taken when the figurehead arrived at the Museum show a weathered carving without feet, base, or hands.

Chapter 5

Looking at Figureheads

Most figureheads in public and private collections today bear the scars of earlier damage and neglect. Some were broken at sea; others were stranded on shore or used as garden sculptures where, without the care of a shipboard crew, they continued to deteriorate. When they were exposed to the extremes of weather the protective layers of paint fell away, the wood rotted, and the carved details became indistinct. Rarely were they cared for as works of art. The mere size and weight of the larger carvings made moving and storing them difficult.

In addition to facing the ravages of the elements at sea and on land, many old figureheads have been subjected to well-intentioned over-restoration. Limbless figures have acquired outstretched arms. Empty hands have been given bouquets of flowers. Faces worn smooth have been repainted with garish colors in unnatural expressions. Figureheads that have been altered to such a degree can no longer be considered entirely authentic or original. However, in spite of changes that may have been made to it, a figurehead usually retains some features that identify it as such.

Figureheads are different from other kinds of wood sculpture, which include architectural figures, cigar store Indians, garden sculpture, portrait busts, and shop signs, in that they were attached to ships. The indications of fastening methods are almost always present on a genuine figurehead. A notch in the base that would have fit over the stem, drifts that would have fastened the carving to the vessel, and a lacing piece on back are all signs that a carving was originally mounted on a vessel's bow, and are not usually present on other types of wood carvings.

85 (left). Figurehead, three-quarter-length woman with scroll base and lacing piece. H. 33 in. (83.8 cm.). Source: Museum purchase, 39.257.

86. Figurehead, Woman with Gold Belt. H. 41 in. (104.2 cm.). Source: Harold H. Kynett, 53.3099.

Except for the small bust figureheads that resemble decorative portrait busts, the general shape and pose of nineteenth-century figureheads distinguish them from other figural sculptures. Full-length figureheads are often in a striding position, one foot forward, clothes swept back, and the head turned upward; the lower parts of three-quarter-length figureheads usually terminate in drapery folds that cover the transition from figurehead to ship stem. Arms are generally held close to the body. The figures usually stand atop or straddle a billethead.

Even if a carving has suffered surface damage it retains its characteristic pose. One example is an unidentified three-quarter-length figurehead of a woman (Fig. 85). Although it is badly worn and has been crudely repainted, the carving has the unmistakable profile of a figurehead. A lacing piece protrudes from the back and there is a notch cut out of the base. When set flat on the floor the figure appears to have an exaggerated swayback, but that curve becomes more graceful if the figure is placed at a slight angle, as it would be on the bow of a vessel. The awkward upward tilt of her head would soften and seem more natural if she were looking up from the stem of a vessel.

A bung on the front of a figure prompts one to look on the back for a corresponding drift or hole. A billethead sawed off across the middle indicates that the lower half of the scroll remained attached to the bow. A lacing piece indicates that the figure abutted a bow timber (see chapter 1, Figs. 12–14). In some cases there have been attempts to obliterate these attachment pieces. A replaced piece of wood on front at the base indicates that there may be a full notch on back. Notches that have later been filled in are usually detectable. The lacing pieces on "Aleppo" (Fig. 69) and Woman with Roses (Fig. 65) have been removed, probably in an attempt to make the figures appear to have been carved in the round.

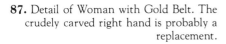
87. Detail of Woman with Gold Belt. The crudely carved right hand is probably a replacement.

Many alterations and restorations can often be recognized with the naked eye. A change in the surface texture around an elbow or shoulder may indicate that an arm has been replaced. A protruding area that would have been vulnerable to abrasion, such as a knee, a foot, or an elaborate head ornament, may show signs of having been filled in. A lack of symmetry, such as that between the delicately carved left hand and the clawlike right hand on an unidentified figurehead, a woman with a gold belt, indicates that some restoration work has been done (Figs. 86, 87). The misshapen right hand is inconsistent with the quality of the rest of the carving and was undoubtedly a later addition. An awkward pose or position, such as that of the Sisters' clasped hands, is a clue that the area has been reworked (Fig. 88).

88. Sisters with awkwardly clasped hands, which are replacements; see also Fig. 80.

Few figureheads exist today with their original paint. Carvings which have deteriorated, but which have escaped being restored, like the Tarkington bust (Fig. 52), are rare. They are, however, of value for the study of figureheads. Paint samples were taken from seven different areas on the Tarkington bust, including the face, hair, dress, and jewelry, and examined under a microscope. Several layers were distinguishable, and all samples showed a base coat of white paint, possibly a lead-base primer. It appears that the figure's dress was originally a pale greenish blue, her hair brown, eyes blue, and lips bright red. Her beads, armbands and dress trim were gold. Later layers are white or pale cream color indicating the figure in later life was covered with a white protective coat rather than repainted in colors.[1]

In X-ray photographs, remaining traces of lead base paint show up as black shadows. Four Seaport figureheads have been X-rayed (see Figs. 64, 84), and the photographs show that on all four carvings most of the original paint, including the primer base layer (lead paint), has been removed. Traces of the lead base mixture usually remain only in the deeper grooves of the carvings' hair or in protected areas, such as behind the ears.

Of the hundreds of figureheads that survive, only a fraction are known to be from specific vessels, and even fewer have been attributed to identified carvers. Figureheads were rarely signed by their makers; the Seaport has no signed pieces. Even figureheads attributed to known shipcarvers, such as the Gleasons of Boston and the Andersons of New York, are unsigned. Five pieces in the collection have words or symbols on them. None of the inscriptions has led to an attribution or identification with the possible exception of the block letters spelling the name on "Orlando."

The task of identifying figureheads is almost impossible. Unless there are obvious indications such as flags, national emblems, or symbols such as crests, eagles, or Indians, national origins are very difficult to trace. Figureheads were seen in ports all over the world, far from the cities and towns where they were carved. A ship of one country might have been built in another country, and the figurehead could have been carved in either. An example is the packet ship *James Baines*, built for the British shipowner of that name by Donald McKay in East Boston, which bore a figurehead made in Liverpool.

Wood type can be a means of identifying national origin. American carvers usually carved figureheads from white pine because it was plentiful and easy to carve. English carvers more often used oak. Figureheads made in India were often of teak.

Comparative studies of unknown figureheads with identified ones in the future may lead to more discoveries. The small bust figures (Figs. 48, 50) that resemble the identified *Eunice H. Adams* figurehead (Fig. 20) may now be assumed to be from American vessels. The large full-length figures (Figs. 51, 67, 69) resembling the *Rhine* and *Balasore* (Figs. 31, 37) carvings can tentatively be attributed to nineteenth-century British vessels. Analysis of carving style, which is possible with fine art sculpture, is almost impossible with figureheads due to surface deterioration.

Often a figurehead has been handed from one owner to another accompanied by a suspect story that it is from a certain coast, or that it is from a specific ship or year. Even when a vessel is identified as a likely candidate, photographs or contemporary descriptions of the carving are needed for absolute identification. Such undocumented stories can clog the files with erroneous data, but in some cases they may present clues leading to identification.

Today few vessels carry figureheads. What was once a common sight is no longer part of the maritime scene. We see figureheads out of context, on a museum wall, far from the bow of a ship. Without a reliable provenance it is difficult to identify them. We rely on the remains of the carvings themselves, as well as on contemporary paintings and photographs, and search for first-hand written accounts.

Almost half of the Museum's figurehead collection is described and illustrated in this monograph. (A list of the entire collection is appended on p. 100.) The figureheads included were chosen because they are positively or tentatively identified or because they are in particularly good, "original," condition and are therefore fine examples of the art.

During the preparation of this monograph two points became apparent. The first is the importance of preserving figureheads without subjecting them to the perils of over-restoration. An unrestored carving, though damaged, can tell us more about how it was constructed, attached to a ship, and painted than one which has been altered by repairs. The second is the value of comparisons. The collecting of information about the Seaport's collection naturally led us to other collections. After scanning countless photographs of surviving figureheads we began to notice striking similarities between some of the Seaport's carvings and those in other collections. As collections are made more accessible through pictures and public exhibitions comparison studies will undoubtedly lead to future discoveries.

89. Figureheads on exhibit in Wendell Building, Mystic Seaport Museum.

Figureheads in the Collection

THE ITEMS IN THIS LIST appear chronologically by date of accession. Those marked with an asterisk are described and illustrated in this book. Titles in quotation marks indicate a traditional but unverified name or attribution. The height given includes the billethead unless otherwise stated.

* "Asia"
  half-length man
  H. 55-1/2 in. (141 cm.)
  Source: Mrs. Harriet Greenman Stillman
  33.41

* Woman with binoculars ("Lady
    Blessington")
  three-quarter-length woman
  H. 37 in. (94 cm.)
  Source: Mrs. Harriet Greenman Stillman
  33.85

* "Orlando"
  half-length man
  H. 68 in. (172.7 cm.)
  Source: Mrs. Harriet Greenman Stillman
  34.83

  "Minnehaha"
  full-length woman
  H. 41 in. (104.1 cm.)
  reconstructed head, shoulders, arms
  Source: Dr. Charles K. Stillman
  36.115

* "Minnie"
  three-quarter-length woman
  H. 33 in. (83.8 cm.)
  Source: Museum purchase
  39.257

  "Lydia"
  full-length woman
  H. 54 in. (137.2 cm.)
  Source: Anonymous
  39.641

  "Wild Goose"
  goose
  L. 33 in. (83.8 cm.)
  Source: Mrs. Harriet Greenman Stillman
  39.2149

* "Drake"
  bust of man
  H. 55 in. (139.7 cm.)
  Source: Harold H. Kynett
  45.642

* "Aleppo"
three-quarter-length man
H. 84 in. (212.7 cm.)
Source: Harold H. Kynett
46.230

* "Mr. Roache"
bust of man
H. 19-3/4 in. (50.1 cm.)
Source: Weston Howland
47.1177

* *Joseph Conrad*
head of man
H. 23-1/2 in. (59.7 cm.)
Source: United States Maritime Commission
47.1948

Woman with jacket
full-length woman
H. 67-1/2 in. (171.4 cm.)
restored
Source: Harold H. Kynett
48.18

Man with high collar
half-length man
H. 71 in. (180.4 cm.)
Source: Harold H. Kynett
48.19

* Woman with comb
half-length woman
H. 44 in. (111.8 cm.)
Source: Harold H. Kynett
48.20

"Thomas Jefferson"
bust of man (possibly not a figurehead)
H. 33 in. (83.8 cm.)
Source: Estate of Frances Alger Pike
48.910

Eagle with shield and portrait
L. 63 in. (160 cm.)
Source: Estate of Frances Alger Pike
48.911

Bust of a woman
H. 31 in. (78.7 cm.)
damaged
Source: Estate of Frances Alger Pike
48.912

* *Great Republic*
eagle
L. 61 in. (154.9 cm.)
Source: Museum purchase
48.942

* "Abigail"
full-length woman
H. 78-1/2 in. (199.4 cm.)
Source: Mrs. Henry C. Taylor,
        Mrs. Albert H. Ely,
        Oliver B. Jennings
48.1133

* *Atalanta*
eagle
L. 81 in. including trailboards (205.1 cm.)
Source: Marian C. Coffin, in memory of her
        mother, Mrs. Julian Coffin
49.753

"Havana"
three-quarter-length woman
H. 69 in. (175.2 cm.)
reconstructed arms and back; probably
  cut down from full-length
Source: Harold H. Kynett
49.756

* *Donald McKay*
full-length man
H. 96 in. (243.2 cm.)
Source: Harold H. Kynett
49.1414

* *Balasore*
three-quarter-length man
H. 85 in. (215.2 cm.)
Source: Powell River Co., Ltd.
49.2853

"Marguerite"
full-length woman
H. 48 in. (121.9 cm.)
extensive reconstruction
Source: Franz Schager
50.140

"Aeolus"
winged bust
L. 42 in. (106.7 cm.)
extensive reconstruction
Source: Harold H. Kynett
50.1713

"Zenobia"
three-quarter-length woman
H. 59 in. (149.9 cm.)
Source: Franklin Remington
50.1722

* Three-quarter-length woman
H. 27 in. (68.6 cm.)
facial restoration
Source: Harold H. Kynett
50.2874

101

* Woman with roses ("Belva Lockwood")
full-length woman
H. 59-1/2 in. (151.1 cm.)
Source: Harold H. Kynett
51.651

Ecclesiastical figure
full-length man
H. 77 in. (195.6 cm.)
damaged
Source: Harold H. Kynett
51.652

Woman with a tie
three-quarter-length woman
H. 26 in. (66 cm.)
Source: Harold H. Kynett
51.3336

Woman with yellow hair
half-length woman
H. 21 in. (53.3 cm.)
Source: Harold H. Kynett
51.3337

Woman with tiara
full-length woman
H. 56-1/2 in. (143.5 cm.)
reconstructed
Source: Harold H. Kynett
51.3338

* Bust of a woman
probably cut down from full-length
H. 35 in. (88.9 cm.)
treated with wax immersion process
Source: Estate of Booth Tarkington
51.3357

* Full-length woman
H. 77 in. (195.6 cm.)
Source: Estate of Booth Tarkington
51.3358

* Rhine
three-quarter-length woman
H. 77 in. (195.6 cm.)
Source: Mrs. Laurence J. Brengle, Sr.
51.4002

Full-length woman
H. 51 in. (129.5 cm.)
reconstructed
Source: Museum purchase
51.4453

Man with crown
half-length man
H. 28 in. (71.1 cm.)
Source: Harold H. Kynett
51.4454

Woman with raised arm
three-quarter-length woman;
    probably cut down
H. 56 in. to raised hand (142.2 cm.)
Source: Museum purchase
52.1203

* "Alexander Hamilton"
half-length man
H. 36-1/2 in. (92.7 cm.)
Source: Harold H. Kynett
52.1205

* Gray man
bust of a man
H. 22 in. (55.9 cm.)
Source: Harold H. Kynett
52.1206

Bust of a woman
H. 25 in. (63.5 cm.)
Source: Harold H. Kynett
52.1207

* Phantom
serpent
L. 91 in. (230.5 cm.)
Source: Harold H. Kynett
52.2110

* Bust of a woman
H. 16 in. (40.6 cm.)
Source: Laurence J. Brengle, Jr.,
        William C. Brengle,
        Mrs. Thomas S. Gates, Jr.
53.87

Man in uniform
half-length man
H. 28 in. (71.1 cm.)
Source: Harold H. Kynett
53.3097

Woman in armor
three-quarter-length woman
H. 47 in. (119.4 cm.)
interior deterioration
Source: Harold H. Kynett
53.3098

* Woman with gold belt
three-quarter-length woman
H. 41 in. (104.2 cm.)
Source: Harold H. Kynett
53.3099

* *Magdalena*
three-quarter-length woman
H. 102 in. (258.4 cm.)
Source: Harold H. Kynett
54.1391

Woman with raised arms
three-quarter-length woman
H. 39 in. (99.1 cm.)
reconstructed arms
Source: Harold H. Kynett
56.177

Woman with flowered base
three-quarter-length woman
H. 46-1/2 in. (118.1 cm.)
reconstructed arms
Source: Harold H. Kynett
56.178

* "St. George"
three-quarter-length man
H. 84 in. (212.7 cm.)
Source: Harold H. Kynett
56.686

Eagle head
L. 29 in. (73.7 cm.)
Source: Charles E. White
U-516

* *Eunice H. Adams*
bust of a woman
H. 17-3/4 in. (45.1 cm.)
Source: Mrs. Henry S. Morgan,
        Charles Francis Adams, Jr.
56.745

* Sisters
double full-length girls
H. 37 in. without base (94 cm.)
reconstructed feet and hands
Source: Mary B. Behrend
57.358

"Merkure"
full-length man
H. 59 in. (149.9 cm.)
reconstructed
Source: Museum purchase
57.386

"Lord Clyde"
full-length man in uniform
H. 60-1/2 in. (153.6 cm.)
Source: Harold H. Kynett
57.875

* *Seminole*
full-length man
H. 76 in. (193 cm.)
Source: Harold H. Kynett
58.632

* *Great Admiral*
full-length man
H. 89 in. without base (225.4 cm.)
Source: Sumner Pingree, Jr.,
        Charles Weld Pingree,
        John R. Pingree
58.1095

* Woman with beads
three-quarter-length woman
H. 74 in. (187.9 cm.)
Source: Mr. and Mrs. Stanley Livingston, Jr.
58.1290

* *Iolanda*
three-quarter-length woman
H. 84 in. (212.7 cm.)
Source: Harold H. Kynett
59.212

Woman in uniform
three-quarter-length woman
H. 51 in. (129.5 cm.)
badly rotted
Source: Harold H. Kynett
59.460

"Lydia"
three-quarter-length woman
H. 38-1/2 in. (97.8 cm.)
Source: Harold H. Kynett
59.461

Woman with fancy hair
three-quarter-length woman
H. 52-1/2 in. (133.4 cm.)
arms badly rotted
Source: Harold H. Kynett
59.462

Woman with laced bodice
half-length woman
H. 31 in. (78.7 cm.)
Source: Museum purchase
63.29

"Molly McKim"
three-quarter-length woman
H. 52 in. (132.1 cm.)
Source: Mrs. Brewster Sewall
64.1

Woman with crown
three-quarter-length woman
H. 38-1/2 in. without base (97.8 cm.)
Source: Mrs. Brewster Sewall
64.2

"Spanish lady"
bust of woman
H. 16-1/2 in. without added billethead
(41.9 cm.)
mounted on added billethead
Source: Boston Yacht Club
64.1696

Eagle
H. 14-1/2 in. (36.8 cm.)
Source: Estate of George B. Mitchell
67.228

Notes

Chapter 1

1. The general history of figureheads, except where noted otherwise, has been taken from the following three sources: M. V. Brewington, *Shipcarvers of North America* (New York, 1972): L. G. Carr Laughton, *Old Ship Figure-heads and Sterns* (London, 1925); Peter Norton, *Ships' Figureheads* (Barre, Mass., 1976).
2. Peter Kemp, *The History of Ships* (London, 1978), pp. 9–11.
3. Hanne Poulsen, *Figureheads and Ornaments on Danish Ships and in Danish Collections* (Copenhagen, 1977), p. 74.
4. Laughton, *Old Ship Figure-heads*, pp. 5, 6.
5. Daniel Ricketson, *The History of New Bedford* (New Bedford, Mass., 1858), pp. 59–60.
6. Brewington, p. 76.
7. Brewington, p. 76.
8. Norton, p. 96.
9. Constance Lathrop, "A Vanishing Naval Tradition—the Figurehead," *U.S. Naval Institute Proceedings*, 53, no. 11 (November 1927), p. 1168.
10. Mabel M. Swan, "Ship Carvers of Newburyport," *Antiques*, 48, no. 2 (August 1945), p. 81.

Chapter 2

1. Marion Dickerman, *The Three Founders* (Mystic, Conn., 1965), p. 7.
2. *Statement of Plan and Purposes of the Marine Historical Association* (Mystic, Conn., 1929), n.p.
3. Dickerman, p. 16.
4. *New London* (Conn.) *Day*, 18 July 1936.
5. Letter, Carl C. Cutler to Clifford Day Mallory, Sr., 21 December 1938 (Cutler correspondence, Museum Archives).
6. Letter, Carl C. Cutler to Fred C. Chase, 25 February 1939 (Cutler correspondence, Museum Archives).
7. Letter, H. H. Kynett to Carl C. Cutler, 13 December 1948 (Kynett correspondence, Museum Archives).
8. Richard C. McKay, *Some Famous Sailing Ships and Their Builder, Donald McKay* (New York, 1928), p. 290.
9. Alain Gerbault, *In Quest of the Sun* . . . (London, 1933), p. 293.
10. Letter, Ricardo Pinto Serradas to Mystic Museum, 28 July 1949 (Registrar's files for 49.1414).
11. "Special Exhibition of Figureheads," *The Log of Mystic Seaport*, 1, no. 1 (October 1948), n.p.
12. "And Sixty Thousand Words," *The Log of Mystic Seaport*, 2, no. 2 (April 1950), n.p.
13. Letter, Carl C. Cutler to H. H. Kynett, 4 December 1949 (Cutler correspondence, Museum Archives).
14. Letter, Powell River Co., Ltd., to Carl C. Cutler, 10 February 1950 (Registrar's files for 49.2853).
15. Letter, Carl C. Cutler to H. H. Kynett, 11 March 1950 (Registrar's files for 49.2853).
16. "The H. H. Kynett Collection," *The Log of Mystic Seaport*, 2, no. 3 (July 1950).

17. "Colgrove Memorial," *The Log of Mystic Seaport*, 4, no. 2 (April 1952).
18. Letter, Elizabeth Trotter to Carl C. Cutler, 2 April 1952 (Registrar's files for 51.3352–3376).
19. "Colgrove Memorial," *The Log of Mystic Seaport*, 4, no. 2 (April 1952).
20. David G. Brierley, "History of the Buildings at the Mystic Seaport Museum," mimeographed manuscript (Mystic, Conn., 1979), "Shipcarver's Shop."
21. Letter, Edouard A. Stackpole to Vernon Smith, Curator, Port Adelaide Nautical Museum, 10 June 1957 (Registrar's files for 58.632).
22. Frederick C. Matthews, *American Merchant Ships, 1850–1900* (Salem, Mass., 1930), p. 288.
23. Jeremiah Holmes, "Dedication of Figurehead of Seminole," *The Log of Mystic Seaport*, Annual Meeting Supplement, 11 July 1958, p. 8.
24. "Exhibits on the Move," *The Log of Mystic Seaport*, 10, no. 1 (Winter 1958), p. 14.

Chapter 3

1. Carol Olsen identified the figurehead from *Eunice H. Adams*.
2. *Bristol* (R.I.) *Phenix*, 11 October 1845.
3. *Bristol Phenix*.
4. Alexander Starbuck, *History of the American Whale Fishery* (New York, 1964), II, pp. 607–633.
5. *New Bedford* (Mass.) *Evening Standard*, 13 September 1902.
6. Pauline Wixon Derick and Barbara E. Goward, *The Nickerson Family*, Part III (The Nickerson Family Association, 1976), p. 263.
7. Letter, Edouard A. Stackpole to Carol Olsen, 23 January 1981.
8. Derick and Goward, p. 263.
9. *New Bedford Evening Standard*, 13 September 1902.
10. *Ship Registers of New Bedford, Massachusetts, 1796–1939* (Boston, 1940), I, p. 22; II, pp. 116, 216, 236; III, pp. 78, 112, 127.
11. Pauline A. Pinckney, *American Figureheads and Their Carvers* (New York, 1940), pp. 124, 126.
12. Letter, Donna J. Christensen, Center for Wood Anatomy Research, U.S. Forest Products Laboratory, Madison, Wisconsin, to Carol Olsen, 1 June 1981.
13. State Street Trust Co., *Old Shipping Days in Boston* (Boston, 1918), p. 46.
14. Richard C. McKay, *Some Famous Sailing Ships and Their Builder, Donald McKay* (New York, 1928), p. 231.
15. A Sailor [Duncan McLean], *Description of the Largest Ship in the World, the New Clipper Great Republic, of Boston* (Boston, 1853), p. 6.
16. A Sailor, p. 22.
17. M. V. Brewington, *Shipcarvers of North America* (New York, 1972), p. 67.
18. Octavius T. Howe and Frederick C. Matthews, *American Clipper Ships* (Salem, Mass., 1926), I, pp. 253–255.
19. McKay, p. 243.
20. Letter, Donna J. Christensen, Center for Wood Anatomy Research, U.S. Forest Products Laboratory, Madison, Wisconsin, to Carol Olsen, 11 March 1981.
21. Carol Olsen examined the *Great Republic* figurehead and noticed it may have originally been longer. Carol Olsen and J. Revell Carr noticed that an auger was probably used to hollow out the mouth.
22. T. E. E. (probably Thomas Edwin Edwardes of *Sea Breezes*), "More about Old Ship's Figureheads," *The Shipping Monthly* (clipping at Peabody Museum, Salem, Mass.).
23. Letter, Ruth O. Selig, National Museum of Natural History, Washington, D.C., to Carol Olsen, 14 April 1981, quoting William C. Sturtevant, Curator of North American Indians, remarks concerning Seminoles.
24. *William Rush: American Sculptor*, exhibition catalog (Pennsylvania Academy of the Fine Arts, Philadelphia, 1982), pp. 97, 124, 172, 176.
25. All of the information on Campbell and Colby was compiled by William N. Peterson and was obtained by me from his article "Campbell & Colby: Shipcarvers at Mystic Seaport," *The Log of Mystic Seaport*, 29, no. 3 (October 1977) and from his personal notes, which he kindly made available to me.
26. *Mystic Pioneer*, 10 March 1866.
27. *Mystic Press*, 19 February 1891.
28. Isabel Anderson, *Under the Black Horse Flag* (Boston and New York, 1926), p. 130.
29. Edouard A. Stackpole, *Figureheads & Ship Carvings at Mystic Seaport* (Mystic, Conn., 1964), p. 7. This attribution is unverified.
30. W. H. Bunting, *Portrait of a Port: Boston 1852–1914* (Cambridge, Mass., 1971), p. 366.
31. H. H. Neligan, "Last of the Yankee Tea Clippers," *Sea Breezes*, 23, no. 226 (September 1938), pp. 203–204.
32. Letter, Isobel L. E. Couperwhite, Watt Library, Greenock, to Carol Olsen, 20 March 1981, quoting *Greenock Telegraph*, 10 December 1886.
33. Basil Lubbock, *Coolie Ships and Oil Sailers* (Boston, 1935; Glasgow, 1935, 1955), p. 94. The other ships are *Main, Moy, Avoca, Erne, Elbe*, and *Volga*.
34. Photocopy of page from cost book for *Rhine*, Russell & Co., sent by Alan Macquarrie, University of Glasgow, to Carol Olsen, 18 May 1981.
35. Isobel L. E. Couperwhite letter; the carvers listed are James Bisset, John Buchan, Joseph Humphrys, Laurie & Fleming, H. N. McFee, William H. Millar, and John Whitelaw.
36. *Boston Herald*, 14 October 1923 (clipping at Peabody Museum, Salem, Mass.).
37. "The Third Magdalena," *Sea Breezes*, n.s. 2, no. 11 (November 1946), p. 335. J. H. Isherwood, "Royal Mail Liner Magdalena," *Sea Breezes*, n.s. 9 (January–June 1950), p. 297.
38. The "ore" ships: *Coimbatore*, 1865, Barclay, Curle & Co.; *Belpore*, bark, 1866, Barclay, Curle & Co.; *Vellore*, 1876, Richardson, Duck & Co.; *Rajore*, 1882, Oswald, Mordaunt & Co.; *Barcore*, 1884, Richardson, Duck & Co.; *Indore*, 1885, D. Richardson; *Balasore*, four-masted bark, 1892, Barclay, Curle & Co.
39. John Parkinson, Jr., *The History of the New York Yacht Club* (New York, 1975), pp. 57, 65, 533.
40. "Register of Vessels Belonging to the New York Yacht Club," pp. 27, 81 (photocopy provided by the New York Yacht Club).
41. Harold A. Underhill, *Sail Training and Cadet Ships* (Glasgow, 1956), p. 55.

Chapter 4

1. Letter, Elizabeth Trotter to Carl C. Cutler, 2 April 1952 (Registrar's files for 51.3352–3376).
2. *Who Was Who in America*, I, *1897–1942* (Chicago, 1962), p. 739.
3. Harold A. Underhill, *Sail Training and Cadet Ships* (Glasgow, 1956), pp. 316–319.
4. Ruttonjee Ardeshir Wadia, *The Bombay Dockyard and the Wadia Master Builders* (Bombay, 1957), pp. 102–105.
5. Entry in *Catalogue of Pictures, Presentation Plate, Figureheads, Models, Relics and Trophies*, published by the Admiralty in 1911, quoted in a letter from Fredericka Smith, Department of Ships, National Maritime Museum, Greenwich, to Carol Olsen, 14 April 1981.
6. *Canopus* and *Ajax* figureheads at National Maritime Museum, Greenwich; *Bellerophon* at Victory Museum, Portsmouth.
7. Wood identified by J. T. Quirk, Center for Wood Anatomy Research, U.S. Forest Products Laboratory, Madison, Wisconsin, 1 May 1981.
8. Wood identified by Department of Scientific and Industrial Research, Forest Products Research Laboratory, Princes Risborough, Aylesbury, England; letter from National Maritime Museum, Greenwich, to H. H. Kynett, 5 December 1960.
9. Letter, Ole Lisberg Jensen, Sjöfartsmuseet, Göteborg, Sweden, to Publications Department, Mystic Seaport Museum, 12 November 1982.
10. Hanne Poulsen, *Figureheads and Ornaments on Danish Ships and in Danish Collections* (Copenhagen, 1977), pp. 93–114, for information on the Møen family. Carol Olsen noticed the comparisons to be made.

Chapter 5

1. David F. Mathieson, Supervisor of Conservation at Mystic Seaport Museum, examined and interpreted the paint samples.

Bibliography

Antiques, 5, no. 3 (March 1924), p. 113, "Editor's Attic." Re: Woman with a Comb.

Altonaer Museum. *Galionsfiguren* (exhibition catalog). Hamburg: Altonaer Museum, 1961. Re: Sisters.

"And Sixty Thousand Words," *The Log of Mystic Seaport*, 2, no. 2 (April 1950), n.p. Re: Balasore.

Anderson, Isabel. *Under the Black Horse Flag, Annals of the Weld Family and Some of Its Branches*. Boston and New York: Houghton Mifflin Company, 1926. Re: Great Admiral.

Archibald, E. H. H. *The Wooden Fighting Ships in the Royal Navy, A.D. 897-1860*. New York: Arco Publishing Company, 1968.

"The Art of the Shipcarver at Peabody Museum of Salem," *The American Neptune*, 37, nos. 1-4 (January, April, July, October 1977), pictorial supplement.

Baker, William Avery. *A Maritime History of Bath, Maine, and the Kennebec River Region*, chap. 44, "The Shipcarvers." 2 vols. Bath, Maine: Marine Research Society of Bath, 1973.

Boston Herald, 14 October 1923. Re: Rhine.

Boston Post, 7 May and 7 October 1923. Re: Rhine.

Brewington, M. V. *Shipcarvers of North America*. New York: Dover Publications, 1972.

Brierley, David G. "History of the Buildings at the Mystic Seaport Museum." Mimeographed. Mystic, Conn.: Mystic Seaport Museum, 1979.

Bristol (R.I.) *Phenix*, 11 October 1845. Re: Eunice H. Adams.

Bunting, W. H., comp. and annotator. *Portrait of a Port: Boston 1852-1914*. Cambridge, Mass.: Belknap Press of Harvard University, 1971. Re: Great Admiral.

Bushell, T. A. *"Royal Mail"; a Centenary History of the Royal Mail Line, 1839-1939*. London: Trade and Travel Publications [1939]. Re: Magdalena.

Casson, Lionel. *Illustrated History of Ships & Boats*. Garden City, N.Y.: Doubleday & Company, 1964.

Christensen, Erwin O. *Early American Wood Carving*. Cleveland and New York: World Publishing Company, 1952.

———. *The Index of American Design*. New York and Washington, D.C.: The Macmillan Company and the National Gallery of Art, Smithsonian Institution, 1959.

"Colgrove Memorial," *The Log of Mystic Seaport*, 4, no. 2 (April 1952), n.p. Re: Shipcarver's shop.

Costa, Giancarlo. *Figureheads: Carving on Ships from Ancient Times to Twentieth Century*. Translated by Brian H. Dolley. Hampshire, England: Nautical Publishing Co., 1981.

Crerar, J. W. "Past Master of a Vanished Craft," *Sea Breezes*, n.s. 3, no. 16 (April 1947), pp. 274-276.

Creuze, Augustin F. B. *Treatise on the Theory and Practice of Naval Architecture: Being the Article "Ship-Building" in the Encyclopaedia Britannica, Seventh Edition*. Edinburgh: Adam and Charles Black, 1841.

"A Day on the Docks," *Scribner's Monthly*, 18, no. 1 (May 1879), p. 32 (illustration of a carver's shop).

Derick, Pauline Wixon, and Goward, Barbara E. *The Nickerson Family, the Descendants of William Nickerson, 1604-1689, First Settler of Chatham, Massachusetts*. Part III. The Nickerson Family Association: 1976. Re: Eunice H. Adams.

Dickerman, Marion. *The Three Founders*. Mystic, Conn.: The Marine Historical Association, 1965.

Dodman, Frank E. *Ships of the Cunard Line*. London: Adlard Coles, 1955. Re: Aleppo.

E[dwardes], T[homas] E[dwin]. "More about Old Ship's Figure-heads," *Shipping Monthly*, n.d., n.p. (Edwardes died 1924). Re: Donald McKay.

"Exhibits on the Move," *The Log of Mystic Seaport*, 10, no. 1 (Winter 1958), pp. 14–15.

Ferguson, Eugene S. "The Figure-head of the United States Frigate *Constellation*," *The American Neptune*, 7, no. 4 (October 1947), pp. 255–260.

Fried, Frederick. *Artists in Wood, American Carvers of Cigar-Store Indians, Show Figures, and Circus Wagons*. New York: Clarkson N. Potter, 1970.

———. "Yankee Figureheads & Their Carvers," *Oceans*, 5, no. 3 (May–June 1972), pp. 57–65.

Fryer, Benjamin N., and Johnson, James. *Bruce Rogers and the Figurehead of the "Joseph Conrad."* San Francisco: Windsor Press, 1938.

Gerbault, Alain. *In Quest of the Sun: the Journal of the "Firecrest."* London: Hodder and Stoughton, 1933. Re: Donald McKay.

Gibbs, Jim. *Pacific Square-Riggers; Pictorial History of the Great Windships of Yesteryear*. Seattle: Superior Publishing Company, 1969.

Griffiths, John W. *The Progressive Ship Builder*, II. New York: John W. Griffiths, 1876.

———. *Treatise on Marine and Naval Architecture, or Theory and Practice Blended in Ship Building*. New York: John W. Griffiths, 1850.

"The H. H. Kynett Collection," *The Log of Mystic Seaport*, 2, no. 3 (July 1950), n.p.

Hall, Alice J. "Legacy of a Dazzling Past," *National Geographic*, 151, no. 3 (March 1977), p. 296 (ship of Cheops).

Hansen, Hans Jürgen. *Galionsfiguren*. Bremerhaven: Stalling Verlag and Deutsches Schiffahrts-museum [ca. 1979].

Hansen, Hans Jürgen, ed. *Art and the Seafarer; a Historical Survey of the Arts and Crafts of Sailors and Shipwrights*. Translated by James and Inge Moore. New York: Viking Press, 1968.

Hegarty, Reginald B., comp. *Returns of Whaling Vessels Sailing from American Ports, 1876–1928*. New Bedford, Mass.: Old Dartmouth Historical Society and Whaling Museum, 1959. Re: Eunice H. Adams.

Hofman, Erik. *The Steam Yachts; an Era of Elegance*. Tuckahoe, N.Y.: John de Graff, 1970. Re: Atalanta, Iolanda.

Holmes, Jeremiah. "Dedication of Figurehead of Seminole," *The Log of Mystic Seaport*, Annual Meeting Supplement (11 July 1958), p. 8.

Hornung, Clarence P. *Treasury of American Design. A Pictorial Survey of Popular Folk Arts Based upon Watercolor Renderings in the Index of American Design, at the National Gallery of Art*. New York: Harry N. Abrams [1972].

Howard, Frank. *Sailing Ships of War 1400–1860*. New York: Mayflower Books, 1979.

Howe, Octavius T., and Matthews, Frederick C. *American Clipper Ships 1833–1858*. 2 vols. Salem, Mass.: Marine Research Society, 1926.

Huycke, Harold D. "The Scottish Lady," *The American Neptune*, 7, no. 4 (October 1947), pl. 35 (unshipping a figurehead).

Isherwood, J. H. "Royal Mail Liner Magdalena," *Sea Breezes*, n.s. 9 (January–June 1950).

Jones, William Tetlow. "Ships' Figureheads," *Munsey's Magazine*, May 1901.

Kemp, Peter. *The History of Ships*. London: Orbis Publishing, 1978.

Lathrop, Constance. "A Vanishing Naval Tradition—the Figurehead," *United States Naval Institute Proceedings*, 53, no. 11 (November 1927), pp. 1166–1168.

Laughton, L. G. Carr. "Figureheads, 1800–1815," *The Mariner's Mirror*, 46, no. 3 (August 1960), pp. 225–228 (written in 1925).

———. *Old Ship Figure-heads & Sterns with Which Are Associated Galleries, Hanging-pieces, Catheads and Divers Other Matters that Concern the "Grace and Countenance" of Old Sailing-ships*. London: Halton & Truscott Smith, 1925; New York: Minton, Balch & Company, 1925.

Levison, A. "A Master Craftsman," *Sea Breezes*, n.s. 5, no. 27 (March 1948), p. 166.

Lipman, Jean. *American Folk Art in Wood, Metal and Stone*. New York: Pantheon, 1948.

Lipman, Jean, and Winchester, Alice. *The Flowering of American Folk Art, 1776–1876*. New York: Viking Press and the Whitney Museum of American Art, 1974.

Lubbock, Basil. *Coolie Ships and Oil Sailers*. Boston: Charles E. Lauriat Co., 1935; Glasgow: Brown, Son & Ferguson, 1935, 1955. Re: James Nourse, Rhine.

McKay, Richard C. *Some Famous Sailing Ships and Their Builder, Donald McKay*. New York: G. P. Putnam's Sons, 1928.

———. *South Street; A Maritime History of New York*. New York: G. P. Putnam's Sons, 1934.

MacLaren, George. *Woodcarvers of Nova Scotia*. Occasional paper no. 10, Historical Series no. 3. Halifax, Nova Scotia: Nova Scotia Museum, 1971.

[McLean, Duncan]. A Sailor. *Description of the Largest Ship in the World, the New Clipper Great Republic, of Boston. Designed, Built and Owned by Donald McKay and Commanded by Capt. L. McKay, with Illustrated Designs of Her Construction*. Boston: Eastburn's Press, 1853.

Marine Historical Association. *Statement of Plan and Purposes of the Marine Historical Association*. Mystic, Conn.: Marine Historical Association, 1929.

The Mariner's Mirror, 4, no. 1 (January 1914). "Notes," p. 27. Re: expenditures on carved work ca. 1700, British.

Matthews, Frederick C. *American Merchant Ships, 1850–1900*. 2 vols. Salem, Mass.: Marine Research Society, 1930.

Mystic Pioneer, 10 March 1866.

Mystic Press, 19 February 1891.

Neligan, H. H. "Figureheads of the 'Great Admiral,' 'Raglan Castle' and 'Mizart,' *Sea Breezes*, n.s. 5, no. 28 (April 1948), p. 192.

———. "Last of the Yankee Tea Clippers," *Sea Breezes*, 23, no. 226 (September 1938), pp. 202–204. Re: Great Admiral.

"New Additions," *The Log of Mystic Seaport*, 2, no. 2 (April 1950), n.p. Re: Donald McKay.

New Bedford (Mass.) *Evening Standard*, 13 September 1902. Re: Eunice H. Adams.

New London (Conn.) *Day*, 18 July 1936. Re: Asia and Orlando.

New York Yacht Club. "Register of Vessels," pp. 27, 81. New York Yacht Club Library, New York. Re: Phantom.

Northend, Mary Harrod. *Memories of Old Salem, Drawn from the Letters of a Great-Grandmother*, chapter 3, "Figureheads." New York: Moffatt, Yard and Company, 1917.

Norton, Peter. *Figureheads*. Greenwich, England: National Maritime Museum, 1972.

———. *Ships' Figureheads*. Barre, Mass.: Barre Publishing, 1976.

Olds, Nathaniel S. B[ruce] R[ogers] on the Joseph Conrad, reprinted from the *Villager*, 31 January 1935. New York: n.d.

Olsen, Carol. "Stylistic Developments of Ship Figureheads of the United States East Coast," *The International Journal of Nautical Archaeology and Underwater Exploration*, 8, no. 4 (November 1979), pp. 321–332.

Owen, Douglas. "The Devonport Figureheads," *The Mariner's Mirror*, 4, no. 5 (May 1914), pp. 145–147.

———. "Figureheads," *The Mariner's Mirror*, 3, nos. 10, 11 (October, November 1913), pp. 289–294, 321–327.

Parkinson, John, Jr. *The History of the New York Yacht Club*. 2 vols. New York: The New York Yacht Club, 1975.

Pennsylvania Academy of the Fine Arts. *William Rush: American Sculptor* (exhibition catalog). Philadelphia: Pennsylvania Academy of the Fine Arts, 1982.

Peterson, William N. "Campbell & Colby: Shipcarvers at Mystic Seaport," *The Log of Mystic Seaport*, 29, no. 3 (October 1977), pp. 66–71.

Pickett, Gertrude M. *Portsmouth's* (New Hampshire) *Heyday in Shipbuilding*. Joseph G. Sawtelle, 1979.

Pinckney, Pauline A. *American Figureheads and Their Carvers*. New York: W. W. Norton & Company, 1940.

Poulsen, Hanne. *Figureheads and Ornaments on Danish Ships and in Danish Collections*. Copenhagen: Rhodos, 1977.

Quincy (Mass.) *Patriot Ledger*, 2 March 1961. Re: Rhine.

Ricketson, Daniel. *The History of New Bedford, Bristol County, Massachusetts: Including a History of the Old Township of Dartmouth and the Present Townships of Westport, Dartmouth, and Fairhaven, from Their Settlement to the Present Time*. New Bedford, Mass.: Daniel Ricketson, 1858. Re: Rebecca figurehead burial, pp. 58–61.

Safford, Victor. "John Haley Bellamy. The Woodcarver of Kittery Point," *Antiques*, 27, no. 3 (March 1935), pp. 102–107.

Samuel T. Freeman & Co., Sale, Chas. T. Jeffery Library (auction catalog), no. 130. Philadelphia: n.d. Re: Drake.

Sea Breezes, 9, no. 85 (December 1926), p. 191. Re: Rhine.

———, 16, no. 152 (July 1932), cover and p. 52. Re: Donald McKay.

"The Seaport's Figureheads Shine in a New Setting," *The Log of Mystic Seaport*, 29, no. 3 (October 1977), pp. 72–73.

Ship Registers and Enrollments, Ship Licenses Issued to Vessels under Twenty Tons, Ship Licenses on Enrollments Issued out of the Port of Bristol—Warren, Rhode Island, 1773–1939. Providence, R.I.: The National Archives Project, 1941. Re: Eunice H. Adams.

Ship Registers of New Bedford, Massachusetts, 1796–1939. 3 vols. Boston: The National Archives Project, 1940.

Sjöfartsmuseet. *Galjonsfigurer* (catalog). Göteborg, Sweden: Sjöfartsmuseet [1982].

"Special Exhibition of Figureheads," *The Log of Mystic Seaport*, 1, no. 1 (October 1948), n.p. Re: Kynett collection.

Stackpole, Edouard A. *Figureheads & Ship Carvings at Mystic Seaport*. Mystic, Conn.: The Marine Historical Association, 1964.

Stammers, Michael K. *The Passage Makers*. Brighton, England: Teredo Books, 1978. Re: James Baines, the carver Dodd, Donald McKay.

Starbuck, Alexander. *History of the American Whale Fishery from Its Earliest Inception to the Year 1876*. 2 vols. New York: Argosy-Antiquarian, 1964. Re: Eunice H. Adams.

State Street Trust. *Old Shipping Days in Boston*. Boston: State Street Trust, 1918.

Swan, Mabel M. "Boston's Carvers and Joiners," *Antiques*, 53, nos. 3, 4 (March, April 1948), pp. 198–201, 281–285.

———. "A Revised Estimate of McIntire," *Antiques*, 20, no. 6 (December 1931), pp. 338–343.

———. "Ship Carvers of Newburyport," *Antiques*, 48, no. 2 (August 1945), pp. 78–81.

———. "Simeon Skillin, Senior. The First American Sculptor," *Antiques*, 46, no. 1 (July 1944), p. 21.

Sutherland, William. *Britain's Glory: or, Ship-Building Unvail'd. Being a general Director, Building and Compleating the said Machines*. 2nd ed. London: A. Bettesworth, 1729.

"The Third Magdalena," *Sea Breezes*, n.s 2, no. 11 (November 1946), p. 335.

Thwing, Leroy L. "The Four Carving Skillins," *Antiques*, 33, no. 6 (June 1938), pp. 326–328.

Underhill, Harold A. *Sail Training and Cadet Ships*. Glasgow: Brown, Son & Ferguson, 1956. Re: St. George, Joseph Conrad.

U.S. Department of Commerce, Bureau of Navigation. *Merchant Vessels of the United States*, pp. 702–703. Washington, D.C.: Government Printing Office, 1927. Re: Rhine.

Vaughan, H. S. "Figure-heads and Beak-heads of the Ships of Henry VIII," *The Mariner's Mirror*, 4, no. 2 (February 1914), pp. 37–43.

Wadia, Ruttonjee Ardeshir. *The Bombay Dockyard and the Wadia Master Builders*. Bombay: R. A. Wadia, 1957.

Wasson, David A. "The Silent Pilots," *The Outlook*, 109 (27 January 1915).

Who Was Who in America, I, 1897–1942. Fifth printing. Chicago: A. N. Marquis Company, 1962.

Zabriskie, G. A. "Ship Figureheads in and about New York," *New-York Historical Society Quarterly Bulletin*, 30 (January 1946), pp. 5–16.

Index

V ESSENS AND IDENTIFIED FIGUREHEADS are listed in italic type; figurehead entries in quotation marks refer to traditional but unverified attributions.

111

Silent Pilots

Typeset in Goudy Old Style
by Mim-G Studios, Westerly, Rhode Island

Printed on Mohawk Superfine Softwhite Text Paper
by Eastern Press, New Haven, Connecticut

Bound by Mueller Trade Bindery, Middletown, Connecticut

Figureheads in the Mystic Seaport Museum collection photographed
by Mary Anne Stets and Claire White-Peterson

Designed by Paul Gaj, Mystic, Connecticut